DATE DUE

Heroism has long been recognised by readers and critics of Roman epic as a central theme of the genre from Virgil and Ovid to Lucan and Statius. However the crucial role female characters play in the constitution and negotiation of the heroism on display in epic has received scant attention in the critical literature. This study represents an attempt to restore female characters to visibility in Roman epic and to examine the discursive operations that effect their marginalisation within both the genre and the critical tradition it has given rise to. The five chapters can be read either as self-contained essays or as a cumulative exploration of the gender dynamics of the Roman epic tradition. The issues addressed are of interest not just to classicists but also to students of gender studies.

ROMAN LITERATURE
AND ITS CONTEXTS

Engendering Rome

ROMAN LITERATURE
AND ITS CONTEXTS

Series editors:
Denis Feeney and Stephen Hinds

This series promotes approaches to Roman literature which are open to dialogue with current work in other areas of the classics, and in the humanities at large. The pursuit of contacts with cognate fields such as social history, anthropology, history of thought, linguistics and literary theory is in the best traditions of classical scholarship: the study of Roman literature, no less than Greek, has much to gain from engaging with these other contexts and intellectual traditions. The series offers a forum in which readers of Latin texts can sharpen their readings by placing them in broader and better-defined contexts, and in which other classicists and humanists can explore the general or particular implications of their work for readers of Latin texts. The books all constitute original and innovative research and are envisaged as suggestive essays whose aim is to stimulate debate.

Other books in the series

Catharine Edwards, *Writing Rome: textual approaches to the city*
Denis Feeney, *Literature and religion at Rome: cultures, contexts, and beliefs*
Philip Hardie, *The epic successors of Virgil: a study in the dynamics of a tradition*
Stephen Hinds, *Allusion and intertext:*
dynamics of appropriation in Roman poetry
Duncan F. Kennedy, *The arts of love:*
five studies in the discourse of Roman love elegy
Charles Martindale, *Redeeming the text:*
Latin poetry and the hermeneutics of reception

Engendering Rome
Women in Latin epic

A. M. KEITH

*Associate Professor of Classics
and Fellow of Victoria College,
University of Toronto*

CAMBRIDGE
UNIVERSITY PRESS

PUBLISHED BY THE PRESS SYNDICATE OF THE UNIVERSITY OF CAMBRIDGE
The Pitt Building, Trumpington Street, Cambridge, United Kingdom

CAMBRIDGE UNIVERSITY PRESS
The Edinburgh Building, Cambridge CB2 2RU, UK   http://www.cup.cam.ac.uk
40 West 20th Street, New York NY 10011-4211, USA   http://www.cup.org
10 Stamford Road, Oakleigh, Melbourne 3166, Australia

First published 2000

Printed in the United Kingdom at the University Press, Cambridge

Typeset in 9.5/12 Times New Roman in QuarkXPress™   [SE]

A catalogue record for this book is available from the British Library

Library of Congress cataloguing in publication data

Keith, A.M., 1962–
Engendering Rome : women in Latin epic / A.M. Keith.
p.   cm. – (Roman literature and its contexts)
Includes bibliographical references and index.
ISBN 0 521 55419 5 (hardback)   ISBN 0 521 55621 X (paperback)
1. Epic poetry, Latin–History and criticism.   2. Women and
literature–Rome–History.   3. Sex role in literature.   I. Title.
II. Series.
PA6054.K44   2000
873′.0109352042–dc21   99-23184   CIP

ISBN 0 521 55419 5 hardback
ISBN 0 521 55621 X paperback

For Esmé,
with love and respect

Contents

ix

Acknowledgments

Slender though this volume is, it has been many years in the making. Its genesis lies in a course on 'women in epic' I taught in the Department of Classics and the Women's Studies Program at the University of Toronto from 1989 to 1996. My students, excited by the large secondary literature on women in Homer, Hesiod, Apollonius and Virgil, challenged me to explore the representation of women in less frequently studied poems of the Latin epic tradition, especially Ennius, Ovid and Lucan. My thanks to Debbie Ellis, Kristi Gourlay, Austra Gulens, Christian Jaekl, Paul Meyer, Kimberley-Anne Pixley, Valerie Walker Smith and Arianna Traill, whose questions and answers started me on the path to the composition of this study. The initial research for the project was undertaken in 1991–92 with the support of a semester's leave funded by the Social Sciences and Humanities Council of Canada. A visiting fellowship to Clare Hall, Cambridge, in 1994–95 provided me with an opportunity to draft early versions of Chapters 1, 2, 3, and 4. It is a pleasure to acknowledge the support of both institutions.

Many people have discussed the issues explored in this work with me and shared their expertise. I presented portions of chapters 2, 3, 4 and 5 at universities and conferences in North America and England and learned much from the audiences on those occasions; especially helpful were the comments and questions of Mark Buchan, Ted Buttrey, James Clauss, Catherine Connors, Mark Golden, Philip Hardie, Stephen Hinds, Martha Malamud, Mark Morton, Sara Myers, Vince Rosivach, and Benjamin Victor. Clifford Ando and Michael Dewar assisted me in elucidating the difficult sequence of thought and compressed expression of the late antique commentators on Virgil and Statius, and I wish to record my thanks to them both. I am deeply grateful to those who generously read and commented on drafts of one or more chapters: Ruth Rothaus Caston, Catherine Connors, Mary Hamer, Philip Hardie, Sandra Joshel, Alex Kurke, Maura Lafferty, Carole Newlands, Georgia Nugent, Alina Payne, Amy Richlin, Jill Ross, Christine Roulston, and Niall Slater.

Denis Feeney and Stephen Hinds have read more drafts than any of us cares to recall, and their critical acumen has improved the manuscript immeasurably. I thank both for challenging me to think through Roman epic in the light of feminist theory. Stephen Rupp read innumerable versions of every chapter, offering searching criticism and constant encouragement throughout the long process of composition. I am deeply conscious of how much my understanding of classical epic has been shaped by dialogue with him.

This book is dedicated to my sister, whose twin passions for intellectual inquiry and feminism have been a challenge and a source of pleasure to me for as long as I can remember.

A.M. Keith
Toronto, 1998

Introduction: gender and genre

From Homer to Claudian, classical Greek and Latin epic poetry was composed by men, consumed largely by men, and centrally concerned with men. The ancients knew of no female epic poets. The Greek 'singer of tales' was a man, whether a fictional character in the Homeric poems themselves (such as Phemius or Demodocus), an exponent of Homeric poetry (such as one of the Homeridae, a Chian guild of bards who recited Homeric poetry in the classical period, or the fictional Ion of the eponymous Platonic dialogue), or one of the mythological or historical singers of non-Homeric epic (such as Orpheus, Hesiod, Panyassis, and Apollonius Rhodius). Ancient and modern critics alike have therefore assumed that behind the name of Homer there lies either a single master poet or a succession of male singers.

A signal exception to this consensus is Samuel Butler, who argued in *The Authoress of the Odyssey* (1922) that the poem must have been written by a woman, so numerous, so sensitive, and so varied are the depictions of female characters in the *Odyssey*. Lillian Doherty has shown that 'what he mistook for evidence of female authorship is actually evidence for the inclusion of females in the implied audience of the poem',[1] but his work gave renewed attention to the integral importance of female characters in the world of Homeric epic, a subject which has been the focus in recent decades of much provocative scholarship.[2] Homer's ancient commentators long ago saw in the web Helen weaves in

---

[1] Doherty (1995), 104 n. 43.
[2] See, e.g., Foley (1978); Bergren (1980) and (1981); Arthur (1981) and Arthur Katz (1992); Felson-Rubin (1994); Doherty (1995); and Holmberg (1995).

the third book of the *Iliad*, depicting the Trojan war as a struggle undertaken for her sake, 'a worthy model of his own poem'.[3] By projecting herself into her tapestry, the Homeric Helen implies that women and their activities are central themes of epic song.[4] Elsewhere in the *Iliad* Helen explicitly refers to her relationship with Paris as a fertile subject of song for later ages (6.356–8), while in the *Odyssey* Agamemnon envisions two competing traditions of epic respectively devoted to the celebration of Penelope's virtue and Clytemnestra's vice (24.196–202).

The Homeric poet in his own voice, however, defines the subject of epic song as the 'famous exploits of men' (κλέα ἀνδρῶν, *Il.* 9.189, 524, *Od.* 8.73), a gender-specific interpretation of the genre echoed by poets and critics for millennia.[5] Throughout antiquity, epic poetry in general (most commonly exemplified by Homeric epic) was viewed as a genre primarily concerned with masculine social identity and political activity, particularly in the context of warfare. In Aristophanes' *Frogs*, for example, Aeschylus attributes Homer's fame to his focus on 'battle order, valour, and the arming of men' (τάξεις ἀρετὰς ὁπλίσεις ἀνδρῶν, *Ran.* 1036).[6] But Homer enjoyed an authority that extended far beyond the conduct of war into all reaches of ancient Greek life. From the archaic period until well into the Byzantine era, Homeric epic served as the cultural template for Hellenism.[7] In Plato's *Republic*, Socrates sketches the poet's central place in Greek culture: 'you hear people singing the praises of Homer, that this poet has educated Greece, that we should take him and study him for the administration and cultivation of human affairs, that we should regulate all our own lives by this poet' (*R.* 10.606e).[8] Plato acutely analyses the close connection

---

[3] Schol. ad *Il.* 3.126–7. On Helen's web, see Bergren (1980).

[4] On the focalization of the tapestry through the character of Helen, see de Jong (1987), 120.

[5] On classical and hellenistic Greek theory about epic, see Koster (1970). Within the *Iliad* itself, the androcentrism of the genre is well brought out in Thersites' abusive attack on the Greek chiefs: 'My poor weak friends, you sorry disgraces, you women of Achaia, not men' (2.235).

[6] Cf. Pl. *Ion* 540d5–541b5; Xen. *Smp.* 4.6, *Mem.* 4.2.10

[7] Marrou (1956), 9–13. Nagy (1979), 5–9, (1990), 36–82, and (1990a), 52–115, argues that the composition of the Homeric and Hesiodic epics in the eighth century BCE was already Panhellenic. Havelock (1963), 61–86, emphasises the central place of Homeric poetry in Greek education and culture.

[8] Cf. *R.* 10.598d-e; *Prt.* 325, 312b3–4; *Hp. Mn.* 365b; *Ion* 531c-d, and 536e1–3.

between the widespread instructional use of poetry and its commemorative function: 'poetry, by embellishing the myriad feats of the
men of old, educates those who come after' (*Phdr.* 245a). Antisthenes,
an Athenian character in Xenophon's *Symposium*, lays bare the gender-
bias implicit in this view when he reports his father's belief that familiarity with Homeric poetry forms the basis of the good *man*'s character
(ἀνὴρ ἀγαθός, *Smp.* 3.5).

As early as the fifth century before our era, Greek sophists began to
charge a fee to train boys in the art of public speaking through the study
of epic and lyric poetry, but instruction is already a feature of the earliest Greek examples of the epic genre. Hesiodic epic, which the Greeks
thought their most ancient literature, has an explicitly didactic purpose,
and markedly didactic passages also appear in Homeric poetry. In the
ninth book of the *Iliad*, for example, Phoenix relates to Achilles the
exploits of Meleager, one of the heroes of old, as a guide to his conduct
(οὕτω καὶ τῶν πρόσθεν ἐπευθόμεθα κλέα ἀνδρῶν | ἡρώων, *Il.*
9.524–5). Homeric heroes characteristically dispense to their juniors or
receive from their elders instruction in points of personal and public etiquette. 'Always be the best and be distinguished above others', Peleus
instructs his son Achilles and Hippolochus his son Glaucus (αἰὲν ἀρισ-
τεύειν καὶ ὑπείροχον ἔμμεναι ἄλλων, *Il.* 11.784 = *Il.* 6.208).
Throughout the *Odyssey*, Telemachus is tutored in the cultural conventions of Homeric manhood by a series of father-surrogates who hold up
to him the examples of his father Odysseus and his cousin Orestes for
emulation.[9] Since Homeric epic occupies a central position in ancient
Greek culture, the exemplary exploits of the well-instructed epic hero
come to be emulated not only by his fellow epic heroes, but also by 'those
who come after'. Thus the actions of the epic hero are interpreted, until
well into the Byzantine period, as models of good (or bad) behaviour, for
imitation (or avoidance) by the student, who is invited by poet and
teacher alike to identify himself as a latter-day Achilles or Odysseus.[10]
Alexander the Great, for example, is reported to have taken his copy of
the *Iliad* on campaign with him (Str. 13.1.27, Plu. *Alex.* 8) in order, as a
modern historian notes, 'to follow in the footsteps of his favourite heroes

---

[9] See Murnaghan (1987), 34–7; cf. Habinek (1988), 196.
[10] Cf., e.g., Plu. *De lib. educ.*; see Bonner (1977), 241–3, and Marrou (1956), 397 n. 14.
On 'interpellation', the process of hailing individuals as subjects within an ideological matrix, see Althusser (1971).

and emulate their deeds'.[11] The rhetorician Libanius, writing in the fourth century of our era, attempts to reconcile the grammarian Nicocles with his former pupil Clearchus by appealing to Clearchus' respect for his teacher: 'Granted that Nicocles is otherwise worthless, he at least deserves respect because he "made you such as you are, godlike Achilles"' (Lib. *Ep.* 1492.2, quoting *Il.* 9.485).[12]

The commemorative function and interpretive conventions of Greek epic poetry were appropriated along with the formal features of the genre by Latin-speaking poets working in an aristocratic philhellenic milieu in mid-Republican Rome.[13] As in Greece so at Rome epic poetry was an exclusively male-authored genre. Quintilian's exhaustive survey of Roman practitioners of the genre preserves no record of a female epicist (*Inst. Or.* 10.1.85–92), nor does the shorter catalogue of Roman writers of epic offered by Quintilian's contemporary Statius, himself an epic poet. In a poem written to commemorate the birthday of the Neronian epicist Lucan, Statius rehearses the names and subjects of Rome's most celebrated epic poets in a brief list that probably reflects the reading practices current in Flavian Rome more accurately than Quintilian's ideal reading list:

> cedet Musa rudis ferocis Enni,
> et docti furor arduus Lucreti,
> et qui per freta duxit Argonautas,
> et qui corpora prima transfigurat:
> quid? maius loquar: ipsa te Latinis
> Aeneis uenerabitur canentem.   (*Silv.* 2.7.75–80)

The rough Muse of bellicose Ennius will yield, as will the sublime passion of learned Lucretius, and he who led the Argonauts across the straits, and he who transforms the first bodies. What? I shall hazard a greater claim. The *Aeneid* itself will worship you, Lucan, singing to the Latins.

Statius opens his roster of canonical Roman epicists with Ennius, the founder of Latin hexameter epic, and includes in the canon Lucretius, who set out an Epicurean cosmogony in his *De Rerum Natura*; the author of an *Argonautae* (a poem about the heroes who sailed with the Argo),

---

[11] Pearson (1983), 46.   [12] Cited by Kaster (1988), 215, whose translation I quote.
[13] Goldberg (1995), 111–34, esp. 123–4, 131–4; and Skutsch (1985), 1–8.

most likely Varro of Atax, whose translation of Apollonius Rhodius, no longer extant, was well regarded by Roman poets and critics;[14] the author of the *Metamorphoses*, Ovid; as well as Virgil, the most celebrated Roman epicist, whose *Aeneid* itself, Statius suggests, will bow before Lucan's masterpiece, the unfinished *Bellum Ciuile*.

Statius' catalogue of Roman epic poets and their poems furnishes the core of texts addressed in this study, for reasons both strategic and methodological. First and foremost, the poems to which Statius refers are still extant, with the exception of Ennius' *Annales* (which survives in several hundred fragments) and the lost *Argonautae* of Varro. Furthermore, we know that the hexameter poems of Ennius, Lucretius, Virgil, Ovid and Lucan were widely read in antiquity both in school and afterwards. Most importantly, these poets echo and re-echo their predecessors' hexameter poems, thereby establishing a self-consciously Roman tradition of epic poetry. In addition to the Roman writers of epic celebrated by Statius in *Silvae* 2.7, this study will address the three complete (or nearly complete) epic poems of the Flavian period: Statius' own *Thebaid*, which was known before publication and quickly entered the canon;[15] Valerius Flaccus' *Argonautica*, praised by Quintilian (*Inst. Or.* 10.1.90); and Silius Italicus' *Punica*.

Classical Roman definitions of epic from Ennius to Statius adapt ancient Greek genre theory to characterise the subject of the genre as the 'greatest accomplishments of the fathers' (*maxima facta patrum*, Enn. *Epigr.* 45.2 Courtney), primarily, though not exclusively, in warfare, as the opening words of Virgil's *Aeneid* imply (*arma uirumque*, 1.1). In the *Annales*, the earliest Latin hexameter epic (?184–169 BCE), Ennius attributes the pre-eminence of the Roman state to her ancient traditions and men (*moribus antiquis res stat Romana uirisque*, 156 Sk), and we are reliably informed that the *Annales* bore repeated witness to the military achievements of generations of Romans. Indeed Ennius seems to have exploited a Hellenistic Greek innovation in the thematic focus of epic – the shift from an individual hero (Achilles or Odysseus) to a heroic collective (the Argonauts) – to pay tribute to the heroic nationalism that built the Roman state.[16] Just as Greek epic examines the panhellenic

---

[14] Prop. 2.34.85, Ov. *Am.* 1.15.21–2, Quint. *Inst. Or.* 10.1.87. Fragments of the poem are collected in Büchner (1982), with commentary in Courtney (1993), 238–43.

[15] Stat. *Theb.* 12.812–15, Juv. 7.82–6. See Dewar (1991), xxxvii–ix, and Curtius (1953), 48–54.　　[16] Goldberg (1995), 111–34.

5

ideals of manliness (ἀνδρεία) and military prowess (ἀριστεία),[17] so Latin epicists from Ennius to Statius scrutinise the conventions of Roman *uirtus* ('manliness') in 'poetry that trains men' by inculcating the 'values, examples of behavior, [and] cultural models' by which Rome won and governed her Mediterranean empire.[18]

If this project necessarily entails an imperial narrative of foreign conquest and external expansion, it also requires a domestic narrative of internal hierarchy and social cohesion, documenting the establishment and maintenance of orderly relations between generations, classes, and sexes. Thus we find, embedded in Ennius' record of foreign conquest, passages which delimit the social contributions of the statesman's confidant (*Ann.* 268–86 Sk) and the good woman (147 Sk), and which underscore the importance of military discipline even when it conflicts with intra-familial loyalties such as those between father and son (156 Sk) or brother and sister (132 Sk). Roman social relations, both foreign and domestic, are also explored by Virgil, Lucan and Silius, who focus in their epics on crucial moments in Roman history, while even those epicists like Lucretius, Ovid, Valerius Flaccus, and Statius, who write philosophical or ostensibly non-Roman mythological epic, constantly engage in a complex negotiation between their subject-matter and Roman themes.[19] Indeed Roman epic, as a genre, can be said to construct a comprehensive model of 'Roman Order'[20] at home and abroad, including relations between the sexes. The prominent social focus of Roman epic invites us to take up the challenge of feminist criticism to 'account for gender'[21] and so to investigate the role of women in Latin epic.

By fusing ancient and modern definitions of the genre – Latin epic is about men; Latin epic is about Rome – we can see that Roman epic (and its critics) neatly enact what Teresa De Lauretis, appropriating Foucault's theory of a 'technology of sex', has called a 'technology of gender'.[22]

---

[17] Nagy (1979) and Hunter (1993), 8–45.

[18] Conte (1994), 83, on the epic projects of Ennius and Livius Andronicus; cf. Bakhtin (1981) on epic.

[19] On Roman national themes in Lucretius, see Nugent (1994); in Ovid, see Feeney (1991), 198–200, 210–20, and Hardie (1990) and (1993); in Flavian epic, see Ahl (1984) and (1986); Dominik (1990); Hill (1990); McGuire (1990); John Henderson (1991), and (1993), 165–7; Hardie (1993); Malamud and McGuire (1993), 210–12; and Malamud (1995), 189–95.

[20] Henderson (1989), 53; cf. Hardie (1993), 3; and Feeney (1991), 276.

[21] De Lauretis (1987), 48. [22] De Lauretis (1987).

Feminist criticism has shown that within every known culture, a symbolic system 'correlates sex to cultural contents according to social values and hierarchies',[23] effectively transforming biological sex into cultural gender. Although the meanings vary from one culture to another, all sex-gender systems are embedded in the political and economic structures of the social order and contribute to the systematic organisation of hierarchies within it.[24] For De Lauretis, gender 'is the product [and process] of various social technologies . . . and of institutional discourses, epistemologies and critical practices, as well as practices of daily life'.[25] Although working principally on twentieth-century cinematic narrative, De Lauretis draws on the literature of psychoanalysis and semiotics – primarily Freud's psychoanalytic reading of Oedipus and Propp's semiotic analysis of folktale (along with Lotman's refinement of Propp) – to develop a theory of the gendered subject in Western narrative and of the process by which subjectivity is engendered in that tradition. Despite the primarily modern focus of her model of 'the work of gender'[26] in criticism and culture, therefore, De Lauretis' work offers a potentially productive means of exploring the 'differential solicitation'[27] of male and female identities in classical epic. In the chapters that follow, I shall examine the questions raised by De Lauretis in the classical Roman context through a series of thematic readings of Latin epic. The role of Latin epic in the context of ancient education (itself a form of elite male social organisation), the particular versions of masculine and feminine identity that Latin epic proposes, and the critical responses that the Latin epic tradition evokes are the subjects of the next chapter.

---

[23] De Lauretis (1987), 5. On the sex/gender system, see Rubin (1975), Ortner and Whitehead (1981), and Caplan (1987). More recent feminist theory has explored the paradox that 'biological' sex is always already culturally constructed, with the result that sex always already turns out on closer inspection to be gender: see Wittig (1986), De Lauretis (1986), and Butler (1990).   [24] See Collier and Rosaldo (1981).
[25] De Lauretis (1987), 2.   [26] The title of Montrose (1991).
[27] De Lauretis (1987), 3.

Epic and education: the construction of Roman masculinity

disce, puer, uirtutem ex me uerumque laborem,
fortunam ex aliis. nunc te mea dextera bello
defensum dabit et magna inter praemia ducet.
tu facito, mox cum matura adoleuerit aetas,
sis memor et te animo repetentem exempla tuorum
et pater Aeneas et auunculus excitet Hector.

(*Aen.* 12.435–40)[1]

Yes, yes, if you please, no reference to examples in books. Men have had
every advantage of us in telling their own story. Education has been theirs
in so much higher a degree; the pen has been in their hands. I will not allow
books to prove any thing.

(Jane Austen, *Persuasion*)

When Statius published the *Thebaid* in 92 CE, late in the reign of the
emperor Domitian, he hoped to secure the lasting success of his epic by
attracting imperial favour and by achieving a place in the Roman educational system. In an unusual envoi bidding farewell to his epic, Statius
records indications of the present popularity of the poem as an index of
its future acclaim: *iam certe praesens tibi Fama benignum | strauit iter
coepitque nouam monstrare futuris. | iam te magnanimus dignatur noscere*

---

[1] 'Learn manliness, boy, and true toil from me, luck from others. Now my right hand
will keep you safe in war and lead you into the midst of great rewards. See to it that
you remember my deeds, when adulthood comes upon you, and that your father
Aeneas and your father's brother Hector inspire you to live up to the examples of
your ancestors.'

Caesar, | *Itala iam studio discit memoratque iuuentus* ('Certainly attendant Fame has already laid a benevolent path for you, and begun to show you, new as you are, to future generations. Already generous Caesar deigns to know you; already the youth of Italy learns you with zeal and recites you', *Theb.* 12.812–15). Statius was neither the first nor the last in the long line of ancient epicists to aspire to a place in the classical curriculum on the model of Homer, whose poetry enjoyed pride of place in education throughout antiquity.[2] Suetonius records that grammatical study at Rome originated with Livius Andronicus and Ennius, both of whom taught Greek as well as Latin in the houses of aristocratic Roman patrons (Suet. *Gram.* 1.2). Livius Andronicus composed a Latin version in Saturnians of Homer's *Odyssey* which was still in use as a teaching text in Horace's youth (Hor. *Ep.* 2.1.69–71), but it was Ennius' *Annales*, the first hexameter epic composed in Latin, which conferred on its author the title of *Homerus alter* and acceded to a position of unchallenged primacy in Roman education during the Republic.[3]

Suetonius reports that both Livius and Ennius made use of their own compositions to teach Latin (*Gram.* 1.2), and passages in Ennius' poetry lend credence to the Suetonian notice. An epigram written to accompany a statue of Ennius, in all likelihood written by the poet himself, celebrates his achievement in the *Annales* in diction that strikingly resembles Aeneas' injunction to Ascanius, quoted in the epigraph of this chapter: *aspicite, o ciues, senis Enni imaginis formam:* | *hic uestrum panxit maxima facta patrum* ('Look, citizens, at the shape of the portrait of old Ennius: he depicted the greatest deeds of your ancestors', *Epigr.* 45 Courtney). This epitaph implies, as Conte has suggested, that the *Annales* 'celebrates the history of Rome as the sum total of heroic exploits proceeding from the *uirtus* . . . of the outstanding individuals, the great nobles and magistrates who had led disciplined armies to victory'.[4] The interdependence of the commemorative and didactic functions of the *Annales* is implicit in the tradition

---

[2] On Statius' didactic program here, see Malamud (1995), 194–5. On ancient education, see Marrou (1956); Bonner (1977); and Harris (1989), 96–114, 129–39, 157–62, 233–49, 306–12. On Homer's centrality in Greco-Roman education, see Marrou (1956), 9–10; Bonner (1977), 213; Harris (1989), 39; and Conte (1994), 83.

[3] Republican writers regularly associate Ennius with Homer (Var. *R.* 1.1.4, Cic. *Orat.* 109, *Rep.* 6.10; cf. Hor. *Ep.* 2.1.50, Sen. *Ep.* 108.34); imperial authors associate Homer with Virgil (Sen. *Dial.* 8.2, Quint. *Inst. Or.* 1.8.5, 4.1.34, 10.1.85, 12.11.26; Juv. 6.436–7).   [4] Conte (1994), 83.

recorded by the elder Pliny that Ennius supplemented his original design of fifteen books with a continuation memorialising recent wars.[5]

Whatever the nature of Ennius' teaching career and however he employed the *Annales* in his teaching, the poem was certainly used as a teaching text after his death. It was expounded to large audiences by Q. Vargunteius in emulation of the rhetorician Crates, who gave public lectures on Greek authors while convalescing from a fall in Rome shortly after the death of Ennius (Suet. *Gram.* 2.2), and as early as the first half of the second century BCE commentaries on the *Annales* began to appear.[6] The *Annales* enjoyed pre-eminence in the Latin curriculum until early in the principate when Virgil's *Aeneid* superseded it as the national epic.[7] Even in the Flavian period, however, the great Roman educator and rhetorician Quintilian, holder of the first chair of Latin at Rome, identifies Ennius as the earliest exponent of epic at Rome and commends the *Annales* as still well worth study (*Inst. Or.* 10.1.88).

This chapter examines the social and institutional contexts in which Latin epic poetry was first encountered and interpreted, in order to investigate the place of epic within the curriculum and the social function of schooling in ancient Rome. In order to analyse the scholastic role of epic in the cultural reproduction of social relations, particularly gender relations, in Roman antiquity, I shall also scrutinise both the explicit statements about the female in Latin epic and the interpretation of these statements in the ancient commentary tradition on Latin epic.[8] Modern sociologists of education agree that 'the systematic regulation of reading and writing belongs to the project of social reproduction',[9] and I shall be particularly concerned to examine the conventions of classical Roman

---

[5] Skutsch (1985), 563–4.   [6] Skutsch (1985), 8–9.

[7] On Ennius' primacy in Republican education, see Skutsch (1985), 9–16, 20–4, 26–9, 34–5. On Virgil's primacy in the imperial period, see Marrou (1956), 252; Bonner (1977), 213–14; and Harris (1989), 29, 227, 261; and on Virgil's continuing centrality in the curricula of late antique and medieval Europe, see Curtius (1953), 48–54, 167–202; and Desmond (1994).

[8] On the sociology of education, see Bourdieu (1977), 187–90; (1984); (1990), 124–5; and Bourdieu and Passeron (1977). Feminist criticism has demonstrated that the importance of canonical texts in the educational systems of a culture derives at least in part from their formulation and perpetuation of culturally prescribed social roles under patriarchy: see Homans (1987), Moi (1990), and Pope (1989).

[9] Guillory (1993), 61; cf. Kaster (1988), 11–14 and Harris (1989), 333–4. My thanks to Georgia Nugent for drawing Guillory (1993) to my attention.

schooling from this perspective. We shall see that ancient Roman educators undertook to school their (mostly male) pupils in Roman conventions of manliness. The ancient Roman grammarian accomplished this goal through linguistic instruction imparted in the form of the exposition of heroic narrative – Ennius' *Annales*, Virgil's *Aeneid*, even, perhaps, Statius' *Thebaid*. Simultaneously, the rituals of the ancient classroom trained elite Roman youths in 'male friendship, mentorship, entitlement, and rivalry', in short, the conventions of 'homosocial' intercourse.[10] The rhetorician built on this linguistic and social foundation, reusing the familiar materials of Roman epic and introducing the student to a host of other genres to teach the techniques of public speaking. In the schools of both grammarian and rhetorician, epic poetry was interpreted primarily as the repository of culturally valued *exempla*, mastery of which set one on the path to the highest social and political positions.[11] Familiarity with Roman epic thus constituted an essential component of the ancient Roman's 'cultural capital',[12] and confirmed his membership in the social and political elite. If it is true, as Pierre Bourdieu has suggested, that 'it is through the teacher that socially recognised hierarchies and our place within them are established',[13] the ancient Roman teacher's exposition of epic will have played an early and important role in introducing elite Roman youth to the social and political conventions of elite Roman culture.

Schools are among the earliest social institutions to which children are admitted on a regular footing in their own right, and second in importance only to the family in acculturating them. As a form of socialisation, Roman schools were distinguished by their reliance on two sources of identity and cohesion, class privilege and homosocial bonding, ritually

---

[10] The concept of 'homosocial bonding' is developed in connection with English literature by Sedgwick (1985), who defines homosociality as 'social bonds between persons of the same sex' and identifies male friendship, mentorship, entitlement, and rivalry as the essential characteristics of modern homosocial behaviour (1).

[11] On the role of the ancient school in the recruitment of the imperial bureaucracy, see Marrou (1956), 310–12; Bolgar (1954), 13–45; Kaster (1988); and Harris (1989); on the ideological implications of this education in the provinces, see Guillory (1993), 60–3.

[12] The term is prominent in the theory of educational sociology developed by Pierre Bourdieu: see Bourdieu (1977), 183–8; (1984); (1990), 124–5; and Bourdieu and Passeron (1977). The concept is treated in relation to the literary canon by Guillory (1993), 3–82.   [13] Bourdieu *et al.* (1994), 13.

inscribed and enacted in the classroom hierarchy. The privileges of class, gender and citizenship were established and reinforced through the use of rituals that effectively promoted hierarchy within the student body and simultaneously excluded the vast majority of the population from the privileges afforded by schooling. An education was available in the ancient world only for a price and was therefore accessible to and practical for only a highly select upper class clientele.[14] Ancient testimony suggests that elite Roman boys and girls were home-schooled before the age of seven, when boys might be sent to study under a *grammaticus*, 'grammarian' (Quint. *Inst. Or.* 1.1.15). Evidence for the education of upper-class Roman women is ample but there is little evidence that they acquired their education in schools; they were more likely to receive an education at home from a private tutor than to attend the grammarian's school.[15] There the male offspring of the elite were schooled in 'the art of speaking correctly and the interpretation of the poets' (*recte loquendi scientiam et poetarum enarrationem*, Quint. *Inst. Or.* 1.4.2).

The grammarian's school was the first step on the path to a wide array of upper class male prerogatives, and constituted the prerequisite for entry into the social and political elites. The ancient school was an important site for the initiation of upper class Roman youths into the conventions of male friendship, as it afforded ample opportunity for the offspring of the social and political elite to learn how to construct and sustain homosocial bonds.[16] In making a case for sending children to school instead of keeping them at home for private tutoring, Quintilian emphasises the importance of social factors in education (*Inst. Or.* 1.2.9–31) and adduces the benefit of 'friendships which last very firmly all the way to old age' (1.2.20).[17] Elsewhere he emphasises the important political benefits to be gained from the induction into social codes of conduct acquired through immersion in them at the grammarian's school: 'Above all let the future orator, who must live in the very greatest publicity and in the midst of the state's spotlight, become accustomed

---

[14] Kaster (1988), 11–14 and Harris (1989), 233–48; cf. Guillory (1993), 60–3.

[15] See Bonner (1977), 27–8, 107; and Harris (1989), 239–40, 252–3, 259. Marrou (1956), 274 nn. 2–7, and Bonner (1977), 135–6, press the evidence for Roman girls attending the grammarian's school; the scepticism of Harris (1989), 239–40 and 309–10, is preferable.   [16] See Kaster (1988), *passim*, especially 13–14.

[17] Cicero's lifelong friendship with Atticus exemplifies the advantages of political and financial support such relationships offered: see Rawson (1975), 12–15, 25–7.

even from a tender age neither to fear men nor to grow pale in solitude like a shaded vine' (1.2.18).

In addition to fostering friendship, ancient schools promoted competition among students, and they thereby functioned as an important training ground for the competition in public speaking that constituted the chief part of a career in law and politics in imperial Rome. Teachers typically used rituals, especially those of competition, age-segregation, and corporal punishment, to construct hierarchies and promote competition among their students. Suetonius reports that the grammarian Verrius Flaccus, for example, made such a name for himself from the efficacy of his pedagogical method that he was engaged by Augustus to teach his grandsons: 'for to stimulate the efforts of his pupils, he used to pit those of the same level against one another, not only setting the subject on which they were to write, but even offering a prize for the victor to carry off' (*Gram.* 17.2). Quintilian was keenly aware of the larger social and political benefits which accrued to the prospective orator from this feature of the educational system:

> Add to this the fact that at home he can learn only those things which are taught to him, while in school he can also learn the things which are taught to others. Every day he will hear many things approved, many corrected, the rebuke of another's idleness and the praise of diligence will benefit him; rivalry will be provoked by praise, he will consider it shameful to yield to an equal, splendid to have surpassed his elders. All these things kindle a boy's spirits, and though ambition itself be a vice, nevertheless it is often the source of virtues (*causa uirtutum*). (*Inst. Or.* 1.2.21–2)

Quintilian reminisces approvingly about his own teachers' practice and promotion of hierarchy, primarily through competitive performance (1.2.23–6), and although he himself deprecates the use of corporal punishment (1.3.14), there is evidence of its widespread use in schooling in antiquity.[18]

This institutional context was the setting for the grammarian's teach-

---

[18] Hor. *Ep.* 2.1.70, Mart. 10.68.11–12, Juv. 14.18–19, Suet. *Gram.* 9.4: see further Marrou (1956), 272–3; Bonner (1977), 142–5. On class-room etiquette and teaching rituals, see Suet. *Gram.* 17, Quint. *Inst. Or.* 1.2 with Bonner (1977), 179–80, and Marrou (1956), 272–3. On the Latin class itself as an initiation rite in the European renaissance, see Ong (1959).

ing of correct speech through the explanation of the poets, which constituted the foundation of the formal education available in antiquity. From
the first rung of the curriculum, epic was intimately implicated in the education of the Roman elite.[19] The close connection between learning to
read and learning epic emerges particularly forcefully from Quintilian's
discussion of *lectio* ('reading' in the sense of 'recitation'), the founda-
tional exercise of the grammarian's school. Quintilian describes in
minute detail the subtleties of the art of reading which the pupil was
expected to master (when to draw breath, slow down, speed up, etc.) but
in his view, the most important part of the lesson lay in instilling in the
budding orator a *manly* tone:

> Let his recitation, however, be manly (*uirilis*) above all, and
> authoritative with a certain integrity, and not at any rate similar to
> prose, since it is poetry, and the poets claim that they sing; nor
> nevertheless let it be loosened into a chant, or become effeminate
> (*effeminata*) by affected modulation, as now happens among most
> people.   (1.8.2)

Instruction in gender difference and the superiority of male over female
was thus a central if implicit feature of the exercise, and one that the
student was expected to internalise.[20]

In this context epic is an obvious choice for primary instruction, since
the genre is pre-eminently concerned with 'the man'. Quintilian enthu-
siastically endorses the prominent position of Homer and Virgil in the
lectio:

> For the rest, they need great care above all that immature minds,
> which will absorb more deeply whatever has sunk into them when
> they are untrained and ignorant of everything, learn not only what
> is eloquent, but rather what is morally good. Therefore the
> established practice, that reading should commence with Homer and
> Virgil, is best, although to understand their merits (*uirtutes*) requires
> more mature judgment; but time remains for this matter, for they
> will not be read once only. In the meantime, let the student's mind be

---

[19] Bonner (1977), 213; cf. Harris (1989), 227, and 261.

[20] Bourdieu and Passeron (1977), 31–54, theorise the (culturally specific) educational
system as the process of inculcating (culturally specific) attitudes and dispositions
in the minds and bodies of its students; cf. Bourdieu (1990), 52–79, on the 'embodiment' or 'incorporation' of symbolic capital.

elevated by the sublimity of heroic verse, derive spirit from the greatness of the subjects, and be imbued with the best sentiments.

(1.8.4–5)

Quintilian associates the inculcation of manly speech in the student with the reading of Homer and Virgil, and implies that youths are schooled in manliness, and away from womanishness, by early exposure to heroic epic. He recommends the study of the ancient poets because they exemplify a stylistic manliness (*uirilitas*) foreign to his own day (1.8.9), and particularly commends Ennius in these terms (10.1.88). Quintilian's lengthy discussion of the *lectio* testifies to the sustained training in Roman cultural conventions of masculinity and femininity that lies at the heart of the exercise. We may accordingly identify the *lectio* as one of the 'technologies of gender' of Roman antiquity, and one, moreover, which employed the epic genre as another.

Upon completing the course of study available in the grammarian's school, the elite Roman youth progressed to the study of rhetoric in a quasi-professional setting that again typically excluded women. At the rhetorician's school, rivalries and friendships among students (and teachers) continued and intensified. The elder Seneca, reminiscing about the declaimer Latro with whom he attended the school of the rhetorician Marullus, records his friend's witticisms at their teacher's expense (*Contr.* 1.*pr.*22), and reports that Cassius Severus, another famous orator of early imperial Rome, compared the rhetorician's school to the gladiator's school (3.*pr.*13). Elsewhere Seneca compares the agonistic setting of the rhetorician's school and the declamation hall to gladiatorial and theatrical competitions (4.*pr.*1), but Quintilian prefers to compare the orator's training to military training: 'Let the orator employ a vigorous and manly (*uirili*) posture of the upper body borrowed not from the stage and actors but from the military (*ab armis*) or even the wrestling-floor' (*Inst. Or.* 1.11.18). Roman rhetoricians cite with approval the elder Cato's definition of the orator: 'The orator, Marcus my son, is a good man (*uir bonus*) skilled in speaking' (Sen. *Contr.* 1.*pr.*10; Quint. *Inst. Or.* 12.1.1). This sentiment, conventional by the early imperial period, implies that successful oratory is predicated less on skill in speaking than on manly excellence.[21] Certainly the elder Seneca judged the quality of a speaker's

---

[21] See further Richlin (1992b), on Roman rhetorical training as training in Roman manhood. For parallel developments in the Greek-speaking part of the Roman empire, see Gleason (1995).

performance on the basis of his performance of masculinity: 'Who among your contemporaries is, what I might call sufficiently talented, sufficiently conscientious; or rather, who is sufficiently a man?' (*immo quis satis uir est?*, *Contr.* 1.pr.9).

Although the student began to read the prose authors required for more specialised training in oratory at the rhetorician's school, he continued to study the epic poets, whom Quintilian deemed of particular use to the aspiring orator because of their focus on the most serious issues of imperial governance.[22] Quintilian emphasises the central importance of Homer and Virgil to the training of the orator by placing them at the head of his Greek and Roman reading lists respectively (*Inst. Or.* 10.1.46–51, 85–92). No longer, however, was the reading of the poets directed towards the mastery of Latin and Greek grammar through exposure to poetic narrative; rather it was directed towards the mastery of rhetorical technique. Quintilian follows Greek oratorical theory in identifying Homer as the first and best exemplar of rhetorical excellence (10.1.46), and he even argues that the teacher of rhetoric should command both the eloquence and good character of Phoenix in the *Iliad* (2.3.12). When he turns from Greek to Latin authors, he compares Virgil's pre-eminence to Homer's, on which indeed it was modelled (10.1.85). Similarly, Aulus Gellius praises the breadth of Virgil's knowledge in the second century CE collection of notes on his reading entitled *Attic Nights* (3.2.14–16), and Macrobius devotes four books of his *Saturnalia*, a fifth-century dialogue about the inheritance of classical culture, to discussion of Virgil's poetry. The *Saturnalia* has an avowedly educational purpose (1.pr.-1.2.1), and tropes its didactic function in the inclusion in the cast of characters of the grammarian Servius, under whose name an ancient commentary on Virgil's works circulated. In the view of Praetextus, the inaugural host of the select company celebrating the festival which gives its name to Macrobius' dialogue, Virgil is skilled in all the disciplines (*Maro omnium disciplinarum peritus*, 1.16.12), an authority equally in all branches of learning and in rhetorical elegance (*poeta aeque in rebus doctrinae et in uerbis sectator elegantiae*, 3.11.9); the fourth book of the *Saturnalia* is devoted to Virgil's mastery of the rules of rhetoric.

---

[22] Quintilian offers powerful indirect support for this view when he commends Stesichoran lyric precisely because it is as weighty as epic: 'his material also shows the strength of Stesichorus' talent, for he sings of the greatest wars and most illustrious generals, shouldering the burdens of epic poetry on his lyre' (*Inst. Or.* 10.1.62).

At the rhetorician's school, the poets were studied not only for examples of rhetorical techniques but especially for examples of epigrams (*sententiae*).[23] Here elite youths learned to hone their skills in the deployment of epigram and wit, whether by culling *sententiae* directly from the poems themselves or merely by becoming familiar with the form: the aspiring orator committed epigrams to memory in order to have an abundant supply on hand when delivering a speech. The impact of the *Aeneid* and the *Metamorphoses* on the oratory of the Augustan period emerges clearly from the quotations and imitations of the two epics in the declamations recorded by the elder Seneca for his sons in the *Controuersiae* and *Suasoriae*. In an anecdote that well illustrates contemporary interest in epic, Seneca reports that the Augustan orator Cestius endeavoured to imitate a Virgilian description of the stillness of night (*Aen.* 8.26–7) for which Varro of Atax had supplied the model (fr. 8 Büchner), and which Ovid imitated in his turn (*Contr.* 7.1.27). Seneca also records his complaint that contemporary rhetoric was dominated by Ovidian epigrams, in a passage showing Cestius himself quoting from the *Metamorphoses* (3.7).[24]

These passages document the declaimers' use of epigrams from epic as a form of 'cultural capital', one of the weapons in the rhetorical armoury of the mature orator.[25] The younger Seneca's prose writings reveal a pervasive debt to Virgilian and Ovidian epic, and furnish valuable evidence about the literary emphases of the education he received from his father and teachers. Quintilian commends in particular the study of Lucan (in addition to Virgil) to the aspiring orator in the Flavian period (*Inst. Or.* 10.1.90), and shortly afterwards Tacitus reports contemporary enthusiasm for Virgil, Lucan and Lucretius (*Dial.* 20.5–6, 23.2).[26] In the heyday of the Antonines, Ennius too, along with Lucretius, enjoyed a renewed popularity, if we may generalise from the interest shown by Marcus Aurelius, who wrote to his ex-tutor Fronto to ask for excerpts from the

---

[23] Epigrams are a major focus of the elder Seneca's works on rhetoric: see, e.g., *Contr.* 1.*pr.*22, 2.*pr.*5, 7.*pr.*9, 10.*pr.*16. On *sententiae* in Roman imperial rhetoric, see Sinclair (1995).

[24] Cf. Sen. *Contr.* 7.1.27, 9.5.17, 10.4.25, *Suas.* 1.12, 3.4–5, 4.4–5. Other contemporary Latin epicists are alluded to or quoted at *Suas.* 1.15, 6.16, 6.26–7.

[25] Cf. Sinclair (1995).

[26] For Lucan's stature in the Flavian period, cf. Mart. 1.61, 7.21, 22, 23, 10.64, 14.194, and Stat. *Sil.* 2.7.

two poets, and Aulus Gellius, who regularly cites both poets in his *Attic Nights*.[27] It is testimony to the prestige of epic throughout the imperial period that quotations from Roman epic, most frequently from Virgil, but also from Ennius, Lucretius, Ovid, Lucan, and Statius, feature so prominently in the Latin prose of the early empire.[28]

In the rest of this chapter, we shall consider some of the implications this culture of reading has for the social construction of gender at Rome in the early empire, by examining passages in which manliness (*uirtus*) is constructed or performed by reference to the female in Roman epic and especially in the *Aeneid*, the most widely read text throughout the period.[29] Valuable evidence about the interpretation of Roman epic poetry survives in the tradition of late antique commentaries on the *Aeneid* and one of its successors, Statius' *Thebaid*. The works of Aulus Gellius, Servius, Macrobius and Tiberius Claudius Donatus are the earliest extant representatives of a continuous tradition of Virgilian criticism that began in the poet's own lifetime with the decision of the grammarian Caecilius Epirota in 26 BCE to teach the works of Virgil and other recent poets.[30] The surviving examples of this tradition exemplify the interpretive strategies to which elite youths were exposed in their reading of the *Aeneid*, and allow us a glimpse of the 'pedagogic work'[31] of reproducing Roman social relations, including gender relations, performed through the reading of epic in the ancient curriculum.

The ideology of Roman *uirtus* pervades the *Aeneid*, nowhere more urgently than in the three great scenes of prophecy that delimit the magnitude of the Roman achievement. The first, Jupiter's prophecy to Venus (1.257–96), elaborates the destiny of Rome in a historical survey of her founding heroes that links myth to the contemporary world of the Augustan settlement. Under the beneficent rule of the historical Roman descendant of Aeneas-Ascanius-Romulus, Caesar Augustus (1.286–8),

---

[27] *Noct. Att.* 1.21.5, 18.5.3; Fronto, *Epist.* p. 105 N; cf. *Epist.* p. 224 N.

[28] Like Seneca in *Naturales Quaestiones* (3.1.1, 3.20.3–6, 3.26.3–7, 4.*pr.*19, 6.13.5, 6.17–18), Pliny the Elder includes Lucretius, Virgil and Ovid among his sources in *Naturalis Historia*. The hexametrical effects with which Livy opens his history and Tacitus his *Annales* also testify to the cultural prestige of epic. For quotations of the *Aeneid* in Pompeian graffiti, see Harris (1989), 261.

[29] Harris (1989), 227, 261, 303; Conte (1994), 284–90.   [30] Suet. *Gram.* 16.3.

[31] On 'pedagogic work', 'a process of inculcation which . . . last[s] long enough to produce a durable training', see Bourdieu and Passeron (1977), 31–54; quote at 31.

Rome will realise Jupiter's promise of empire without end (*imperium sine fine dedi*, 1.279) and mastery of the world (*Romanos, rerum dominos*, 1.282). The imperial destiny of Rome is predicated upon the successive generations of the Julian family, son following father and acceding to manhood in regular succession.[32] Similar exemplary tableaux of Roman *uirtus*, exemplifying male generational renewal conjoined with military glory and expansion of empire, occur in the pageant of heroes in the underworld (6.756–892) and on the shield of Aeneas (8.626–731).

Female characters are conspicuously absent from the scenes that survey the panorama of Roman imperial history in the *Aeneid*,[33] but comparison with the female nonetheless offers one important standard against which *uirtus* is measured throughout the poem. The battlefield vaunt of Numanus Remulus in book 9, for example, is predicated on the differentiation of male from female. Describing at length the hardship in which the Italians live, Numanus explains their hardiness in battle, their true manliness, as the result of this upbringing (9.603–13), and taunts Ascanius that the Trojans' clothing and pastimes betray their effeminacy.

> uobis picta croco et fulgenti murice uestis,
> desidiae cordi, iuuat indulgere choreis,
> et tunicae manicas et habent redimicula mitrae.
> o uere Phrygiae, neque enim Phryges, ite per alta
> Dindyma, ubi adsuetis biforem dat tibia cantum.
> tympana uos buxusque uocat Berecyntia Matris
> Idaeae. sinite arma uiris et cedite ferro. (9.614–20)

Your clothing is decorated with yellow and gleaming purple. Indolence is your delight; you enjoy indulging in dancing; your tunics have long sleeves and your bonnets have ribbons. Yes you Phrygians are really women not men; go along the summits of Dindyma, where the flute plays the two-note song to you who are accustomed to it. The tambourines and Berecynthian flute of the Idaean mother summon you. Leave arms to men, and refrain from the sword.

---

[32] On the theme of succession in the *Aeneid* and Roman epic, see Lee (1979) and Hardie (1993), 88–119.

[33] On the androcentrism of the imperial project in the *Aeneid*, see the exemplary discussions of Perkell (1981) and Nugent (1992).

Numanus' speech draws on a Homeric passage in which Thersites impugns the bravery of the Achaean commanders by calling them women (*Il.* 2.235–6; cf. 7.96, 8.163). The Roman poet has complicated his Homeric model, however, by embedding the misogynistic taunt in an orientalising framework: Numanus, the hardy Italian, insults Ascanius as an effeminate Phrygian.[34] Virgil thus maps the normative sexual hierarchy of Homeric epic onto an orientalist dichotomy that contrasts virile West with effeminate East. He disrupts the force of these mutually-implicated stereotypes, however, when Ascanius easily kills his Italian opponent (9.632–7). Apollo, watching over the Trojan prince, explicitly confirms his manly achievement in a tribute that gestures to the etymological derivation of *uirtus* from *uir* as it implies Ascanius' passage from boyhood to manhood (*macte noua uirtute, puer*, 'congratulations on your new manhood, boy', 9.641).[35] Moreover elsewhere in the poem, Virgil's characterisation of the Trojans as a hardy people (*duri*, 3.94–5, 9.468; cf. 5.729) contradicts the ascription of feminine softness (*mollitia*)[36] to the Trojans implicit in Numanus' assertion of Italian hardihood (*durum genus*, 9.603). In proving Numanus comprehensively wrong in his assumptions, the poet undermines (if he does not finally demolish) the orientalist dichotomy that subtends his character's speech; but the hierarchy of gender cannot be so fully dismantled in a contest which has been between men all along.[37] Since both combatants are male, comparison with the female constructs them not as feminine but as effeminate.

In contrast to Virgil, who calls into question the stereotypes of gender and ethnic character that animate the passage, ancient critical commentary emphasises the dichotomies that structure Numanus' speech and affirms the 'natural' hierarchy of nations and sexes. Servius remarks that the passage constitutes 'invective against the Trojans, in which [Numanus] uses proofs such as Cicero records in his rhetorical writings,

---

[34] The orientalist discourse that undergirds Numanus' speech is well discussed in Horsfall (1971), and Hardie (1994), 185–98, esp. 196.

[35] Hardie (1994), 206; O'Hara (1996), 221.

[36] Varro (*apud* Lact. *Opif.* 12.17) derived *mulier* ('woman', 'wife') from *mollis* ('soft'); cf. Isid. *Orig.* 11.2.18. On the connotation of 'effeminacy' in *mollitia* when applied to men, see Edwards (1993), 63–97.

[37] The Trojan group in Italy is, in theory, exclusively male after the Trojan women are abandoned in Sicily (5.767–71); but cf. 9.473–502, and 11.35.

from nation, dress, bearing, and character'.[38] Although the grammarian does not include sex in this list, he is fully alive to the defamatory purpose of Numanus' deployment of gender stereotypes in his description of the Trojans' clothing. Commenting on line 616, Servius explains that the poet 'was on the point of saying "you have ribands on your felt caps", but he changes that into a greater censure by saying "your bonnets have ribbons". For felt caps are worn by men, but head-dresses by women'.[39] Servius recognises that the core of Numanus' taunt lies in the word *Phrygiae* (9.617): 'he had rebuked them already as "Phrygian" (*Phryges*), and now he says "Phrygian women" (*Phrygiae*) and not "Phrygian men" (*Phryges*) for a greater insult'. In his comments, Servius elaborates and endorses the essential superiority of male over female (and west over east).

Further illustration of the interpretive practices of ancient readers of epic is available in Tiberius Claudius Donatus' *Interpretationes Vergilianae*, an early fifth-century prose paraphrase of the *Aeneid* dedicated to the author's son. Like Servius, Donatus focuses on the normative hierarchy of gender implicit in Numanus' speech when he comes to comment on the Italian's encounter with Ascanius. For Donatus, Numanus' description of the Trojans' clothing is of crucial importance to the interpretation of the passage, 'for a delicate type of clothing brings forth dissipation of mind and body. Then [the poet] shows that decadence of clothing accompanies many vices' (2.268.18–20).[40] Donatus draws on the same sartorial norms of gender difference to explicate Numanus' reference to the Trojan predilection for dancing: 'Shameful dancing goes along with your clothing and a ditty suitable for women, whom you're imitating' (2.268.21–2). The Trojans' clothing is culturally coded in ancient Rome as quintessentially female: 'To such an extent is nothing among you characteristic of men (*usque adeo in uobis uirorum nihil est*), that instead of tunics you have long-sleeved clothing and a head-dress

---

[38] I cite Servius from the Harvard edition, Rand *et al.* (1946) and Stocker *et al.* (1965), for *Aeneid* 1–5 and from Thilo and Hagen (1884) for *Aeneid* 6–12.

[39] Cf. Lactantius Placidus on Stat. *Theb.* 9.795: VERTICE MITRAS mitra est incuruum pilleum, de quo dependent buccarum tegmina. et oratorie crimen obiectum est ex habitus qualitate. Virgilius <Aen. IX 616>: 'et tunicae manicas et habent redimicula mitrae'.

[40] I follow Starr (1991), in citing Donatus from the Teubner edition of Georgii (1905–6) by volume, page and line number.

instead of a helmet' (2.268.23–5). Like Servius, Donatus recognises that Numanus' invective against the Trojans mobilises a conventional hierarchy of gender that deems it demeaning for men to play the (culturally scripted) part of women:

> They err, he says, whoever calls you men and not women of Phrygia; for between you and your women there is no difference at all, you share the same dress, the same bodily weakness, the same mental decadence. To you belongs the greatest contest to outdo your women by striving in pursuit of disgrace. (2.268.25–30)

Donatus' testimony coheres with that of Servius in its ascription of effeminacy to the Trojans on the basis of their dress and behaviour. Emphasising the association of shame and decadence not only with female clothing but simply with the female, he offers a summary of the passage that constitutes a fine analysis of the rhetoric of misogyny animating Numanus' speech. Donatus' paraphrase shows how Numanus, by denigrating the Trojan soldiers for wearing clothing marked as female at Rome, symbolically regenders them as the weaker sex by ascribing to them the 'essential' characteristics of the female: bodily weakness and mental dissolution.

Pedagogical theorists from Quintilian to Bourdieu have argued that students internalise most completely the values to which their earliest schooling exposes them, and have concluded that early and frequently repeated instruction is the most effective in ensuring the 'durability' of the training.[41] We should therefore expect the Roman grammarians' inculcation of this 'natural' hierarchy of gender – true masculinity contrasted with the shameful weakness characteristic of the female – to be particularly long-lasting in view of its conjunction with the lesson in manhood imparted in the *lectio*. The durability of their lessons is visible to us in a passage from the sixth book of Aulus Gellius' *Attic Nights*, where he treats the history of long- and short-sleeved tunics in ancient Rome:

> It was deemed inappropriate at Rome and in the whole of Latium for a man to wear tunics extending beyond the arms, down to the tops of the hands and nearly to the fingers. Our ancestors called

---

[41] Quint. *Inst. Or.* 1.8.5, quoted above; Bourdieu and Passeron (1977), 31–54, on 'habitus', the disposition produced through durable training.

these tunics by a Greek word 'chirodytes', and thought seemly for women alone the clothing that extended far and wide towards the elbows and the shins, to cover them from the gaze of onlookers. But Roman men indeed at first were clothed in the toga alone without tunics at all; later they wore short tunics drawn up to hang down short of the shoulders, the kind which the Greeks call sleeveless.

(6.12.1–3)

Gellius organises this history around a gendered and ethnocentric dichotomy that differentiates Roman men, who wear short-sleeved tunics, from women and foreigners, who wear long-sleeved tunics. After reporting an anecdote concerning Scipio Aemilianus, the exemplary hero of the mid-Republic, Gellius concludes the chapter with quotations from the *Aeneid* and the *Annales* (enjoying renewed critical esteem in this period) that illustrate these dichotomies: 'Virgil too denounces tunics of this kind as if they were typical of women and disgraceful: "and your tunics", he says, "have long sleeves and your bonnets have ribbons". Quintus Ennius too seems to have referred to the Carthaginians' "tunic-clad youth" not without insult' (6.12.6–7). Gellius introduces both quotations to endorse the hierarchies of gender (male over female) and nationality (Roman over foreigner) that he constructs in the course of this discussion, drawing on Rome's two most eminent nationalist epic poets for the final word on the supremacy of the elite Roman male. This conclusion is clearly indebted to Gellius' rhetorical training in the deployment of epigrams drawn from epic for its impact.

The importance of the social differentiation between male and female emerges clearly from examination of the epic usage of *femina* and its cognates, the 'marked' category in contrast to the 'unmarked' *uir*, subject and norm of the epic genre in general and the *Aeneid* in particular.[42] Dido is introduced by Venus, for example, as the commander of the force that founds Carthage, and yet a woman: *dux femina facti* ('the leader of the expedition was a woman', 1.364). Servius' comment on the half-line is, of course, instructive, and should be interpreted in the light of Quintilian's detailed directions about how to read aloud: '[the phrase] should be

---

[42] The central importance of 'the man' in epic is sounded in the proems to the Roman epics and in Latin descriptions of epic: Vir. *Ecl.* 6.3; Vir. *Aen.* 1.1; Ov. *Am.* 1.1.1; Hor. *AP* 73; Luc. 1.1–4; V.Fl. 1.11–12; Stat. *Theb.* 1.41; Stat. *Ach.* 1.3; Sil. 1.1, 5–6. See further Bloch (1970), and Koster (1970), 124–40, on Roman definitions of epic.

uttered as if astonishing'. Donatus offers still less charitable comment: 'Certainly we can also understand that this was included to mock Pygmalion' (1.80.2–3). To Donatus' androcentric gaze, the effectiveness of a female leader necessarily implies the concomitant inadequacy of the male who should master her.

The Dido episode concludes with two gnomic generalisations about the female that align the Carthaginian queen with the rest of her sex and are far from complimentary. The first is the famous line that Dryden called 'the sharpest satire, in the fewest words, ever made on womankind':[43] *uarium et mutabile semper | femina* ('a fickle and ever-changing thing is woman', 4.569–70). As Pease remarks, 'the neuter is clearly contemptuous: woman is viewed less as a person than as a physical phenomenon'.[44] Despite the brilliance of Mercury's epigram, no extant ancient commentator discusses this *sententia*. A passage in the late antique *Origines* by Isidore of Seville, however, illustrates the use to which this Virgilian *sententia* could be put.[45] In an extensive discussion of the classical Roman law court, Isidore catalogues the six people who participate, briefly defining judge, plaintiff and defendant before turning to consider the witnesses in more detail (18.15.6–10). Explaining that witnesses are judged according to their situation, nature and way of life, he justifies each with a sentence of qualification.

> By situation [is meant] if free not slave. For often the slave
> suppresses evidence of the truth out of fear of his master. By nature,
> if a man not a woman. For 'a fickle and ever-changing thing is
> woman'. By life, if blameless and irreproachable in deed. For if a
> good life is wanting, the witness will lack trustworthiness. For
> indeed justice can have no alliance with the criminal.   (18.15.9)

Isidore (following his sources?) cites the Virgilian epigram in order to discredit female witnesses. Although citizen women did in fact enjoy the legal right to appear as witnesses in classical Roman courts of law, Isidore's comment suggests that their credibility might be easily impugned.[46]

Ancient commentary on the conclusion of the Dido episode reveals a

---

[43] Cited by Pease (1935), 460.   [44] Pease (1935), 460; cf. Lyne (1989), 49–50.

[45] Brehaut (1912), 15–88, discusses Isidore's preservation of the classical heritage in *Origines* and demonstrates that he is likely to be a reliable witness to the uses his sources (many no longer extant) made of poetic epigrams.

[46] Cf. Gardner (1995); see Marshall (1989), 51 n. 49 and (1990), 356–7, on trials in which women acted as witnesses.

coherent pattern of assumptions about the female character in broad accord with Isidore's interpretation of Mercury's epigram. As Dido's city burns, Aeneas sails away holding steadfast to his course and, by metonymy, to his purpose (*interea medium Aeneas iam classe tenebat | certus iter fluctusque atros Aquilone secabat*, 5.1–2). The contrast which the steadfast Aeneas presents to the changeable Dido[47] exemplifies a consistent pattern of antithesis between male and female in the *Aeneid* which the commentary tradition emphasises and endorses, taking as their cue the hero's reflection on the flames visible in Carthage: *quae tantum accenderit ignem | causa latet; duri magno sed amore dolores | polluto, notumque furens quid femina possit, | triste per augurium Teucrorum pectora ducunt* ('the source which kindled that great fire lies hidden; but the thought of the harsh griefs of a great love foresworn and the knowledge of what a passionate woman can do lead the Trojans' thoughts to gloomy conjecture', 5.4–7). The ancient commentators are quick to observe and expand the generalising force of the noun *femina* here. Thus Servius glosses *Aen.* 5.6 with the phrase 'the well known madness of women', moving from Virgil's gnomic 'this is what a raging woman is like' to the generalisation that takes in all women, 'this is what women are like, *viz.* raging'. Similarly, Donatus moves in his commentary from general principles concerning female character into summary of the specific situation of Dido and back again to interpretation of the passage according to general principles concerning female nature:

> For it was known from examples that teach what the bitterness of grief can lead to in cases of this sort, what criminal action can arise when love is harmed, what a woman plans when in addition to the weakness of her sex she is overcome by the passion of love. Thinking of these things, the Trojans interpret the blaze as a portent that some evil has occurred in the city in connection with Dido's welfare. . . Virgil wishes to show that women's grief, especially in the case of love, is more serious: for as little as they can do to return vengeance on account of the weakness of their sex, with so great a penalty do they turn upon themselves what they cannot exact from another. (1.425.22–426.7)

---

[47] Lyne (1989), 51, notes that Ovid's Dido throws the charge of changeability back at Aeneas (*Her.* 7.51), and Denis Feeney comments (*per litteras*) that 'Dido herself confutes the slur 25 lines later, when she refuses to *change* her resolve to die (*Aen.* 4.595)'.

Traditional Roman contempt for the 'weaker' sex animates Donatus' paraphrase of the passage: *leuitas* and *infirmitas* delimit the narrow range of his expectations for women.[48] He articulates these limited (and limiting) assumptions in a necessarily circular argument: women's well-known weakness, particularly when they are in love, is adduced in explanation for the fire raging in Dido's city in order that the fire itself can be cited as an example of women's well-known weakness. Throughout his commentary on the poem, he assumes weakness to be the defining characteristic of the female, and not only when in love. In his comments here and elsewhere, Donatus reflects and magnifies the misogyny inscribed in the epic tradition.

Richard Heinze briefly noted the extent to which the female characters in the *Aeneid* illustrate the truth of the generalisations about *femina* in the poem (including those in the Dido episode),[49] and this is consistently stressed in the ancient commentaries. The instability of the female is exemplified at the end of book 5 when the Trojan women set fire to their own ships. The episode is predicated on the gendered division of the Trojan exiles: while the men celebrate funeral games for Anchises, the women lament his death by the ships.[50] Commenting on 5.613–16, lines which describe the universality of the sentiments animating the women, Donatus remarks that everything conspired to offer the opportunity for disaster: 'All things helped with the opportunity for harm: first, the isolation of the place, also a time when the men were absent, even the character of women who can easily be persuaded and whose weak intellect can more easily be led in whatever direction' (1.493.2–6). In Donatus' view, women's weak and compliant nature renders them more fit to be led than to lead, an essentialising assessment of female character that confirms and endorses the social fact of male dominance. His generally low estimate of female nature provides him with an easy explanation for the Trojan women's action, which in turn justifies the decision of the Trojan leadership to abandon the women, the old and the infirm (who are feminised by implication), on Sicily. Thus he endorses Virgil's constitution of the Trojan group that will continue on to Italy as 'the young, the strong, the male' (*lectos iuuenes, fortissima corda, Aen.* 5.729).[51]

---

[48] Cf. Starr (1991), 27.   [49] Heinze (1993), 220–1 [= (1915), 268–9].
[50] Nugent (1992), 267.
[51] Nugent (1992), 274. On this passage, see further Nugent (1992), 267–78.

Camilla furnishes a particularly complex example of the representation of *feminae* in the *Aeneid* and their reception in the ancient commentaries. Virgil emphasises the transgression of gender norms entailed by a woman's participation in the male arena of warfare both in her introduction in the emphatic final position of the Italian catalogue in book 7 and in her aristeia and death in book 11. By introducing Camilla as *bellatrix* (7.805), the poet implicitly aligns her with the Amazon warrior Penthesilea (*bellatrix*, 1.493) with whom he later explicitly compares her (11.662). Virgil signals the extraordinary incursion of a woman into the male arena of warfare in a line that begins and ends with gender-marked diction: *bellatrix, non illa colo calathisue Mineruae | femineas adsueta manus, sed proelia uirgo | dura pati cursuque pedum praeuertere uentos* ('a warrior-maiden, who had not turned her woman's hands to Minerva's distaff and wool-baskets, but rather was accustomed, though a maiden, to endure hard battles and outstrip the winds in the footrace', 7.805–7). The entry of a woman into the catalogue of Italian warriors clearly disturbs the gender code of Virgilian epic discourse, marked as masculine at the outset (*arma uirumque cano*, 1.1) and again at the opening of the seventh book (*acies . . . reges*, 7.42). The collocation *proelia uirgo | dura*, in particular, calls into question the convention of feminine *mollitia* in its transgression of the norms of gender and genre.

In his paraphrase of this passage, Donatus follows Virgil in drawing attention to the impropriety of Camilla's entry into the arena of battle through oxymoron: 'she made over her womanly hands to manly pursuits from the despised tasks of wool and distaff' (2.108.8–9). Elsewhere, however, the commentary tradition processes the figure of Camilla in such a way as to minimise features which might disturb gender norms, and to generate and emphasise elements which are congruent with sexual stereotypes. Servius, who infers that the inclusion of a woman among the Italian forces portends their defeat, commends Virgil for his relegation of Camilla to the final position in the catalogue:

Wisely [the poet] moves on to women after full commemoration of men; for so do we read of the Trojans, who demanded the aid of the Amazons last: an affair which was passed over by Homer. Clearly there is already the hint of an unlucky outcome in the fact that among these very beginnings even women are mobilised under arms.

Both commentators emphasise the amazement Camilla's presence provokes in male and female onlookers alike (7.812–13). Servius comments that 'each sex wonders at the things that have been depicted contrary to their expectation, so that women wonder at arms on a woman, men at such dress on a warrior' (cf. Donatus 2.108.24–5), while Donatus asks 'to what woman or man would it not be miraculous for the manliness of Mars to dwell in the female sex?' (2.108.25–7).

The anxious critical commentary provoked by the initial description of Camilla recurs in the commentators' discussions of her aristeia. Virgil signals her transgression of gender norms by drawing attention to her sex (11.507, 664, 705, 734, 808), characterising her weapons as 'womanly' (11.687) and her behaviour on the battlefield as 'feminine' (11.782). He even surrounds her with a force of warrior-maidens (11.655–8) on the model of the Amazons (11.659–63) in a passage that coheres uneasily with earlier references to her presumably male Volscian troops (*agmen equitum*, 7.804; *Volscorum acie*, 11.498). The emphasis on gender deviance is particularly striking in Camilla's own reference to her 'woman's weapons', the sole appearance of the adjective *muliebris* in the Virgilian corpus: *aduenit qui uestra dies muliebribus armis | uerba redargueret* ('the day has arrived that will refute your words with a woman's weapons', 11.687–8). Servius carefully explains that Virgil uses *muliebris* here not in the strict sense of 'belonging to a married woman' but in the looser sense of 'belonging to the female sex', and Donatus paraphrases 'recognise that you are now such that women can conquer you, women kill you' (2.519.21–2). Donatus underscores the shame inherent in this inversion of the natural hierarchy of gender in his commentary on Camilla's vaunt: 'She herself out of anger deprecates her own action by saying that it is a great disgrace for men to die by a woman's arms . . . for she says you receive the greatest reproach because a woman brought you to death' (2.519.24–30).

Virgil attributes Camilla's death to her reckless desire for the spoils of battle, a desire which he characterises as typically female:

> hunc [i.e. Chlorea] uirgo, siue ut templis praefigeret arma
> Troia, captiuo siue ut se ferret in auro
> uenatrix, unum ex omni certamine pugnae
> caeca sequebatur totumque incauta per agmen
> femineo praedae et spoliorum ardebat amore   (11.778–82)

28

Chloreus alone the maiden hunted, blind to all the contest of the battle and she followed him heedlessly through the whole of the armed ranks, whether to dedicate his Trojan arms in the temples, or to vaunt herself in captured gold; she was ablaze with a woman's love of booty and spoils.

Modern critics have eschewed comment on the adjective *femineo* here despite, or perhaps because of, the fact that it signals the crucial importance of gender difference to the epic world view by proposing an absolute opposition between male and female. This opposition – whether transgressed, problematised, or upheld – is central to Roman epic decorum, however, and the ancient commentators recognise it as such, for they not only note the gender dynamic of these verses but draw out the implications at some length. Servius' gloss emphasises the connotative and ideological, rather than denotative and logical, force of the adjective: 'CHARACTERISTIC OF THE FEMALE in the sense of impatient, irrational, as in "feminine anger and anxiety provoked Amata to the boiling point"' (quoting *Aen.* 7.345). Although Camilla's desire for booty is congruent with the tradition descending from Homeric epic in which a warrior's winnings on the battlefield quite literally figure his heroic worth, Servius interprets Virgil's adjective *femineo* (11.782) as a cue that her interest in Chloreus' rich battle dress, which receives lengthy and lavish description from the poet (11.768–77), is excessive and irrational.

Servius here has recourse to a Greco-Roman stereotype regarding women's excessive interest in clothing and personal adornment. The historian Livy, Virgil's contemporary, articulates a traditional connection between women and lavish attire in his version of a speech in support of the repeal of a Republican sumptuary law:

[Roman] women can partake of neither magistracies, nor priesthoods, nor triumphs, nor badges of office, nor gifts, nor spoils of war; elegance, finery and beautiful clothes are women's badges, in these they rejoice and take pride, this our ancestors called women's world.   (34.7.8–9)

Donatus interprets the Virgilian passage in precisely this frame of reference, recognising and deprecating in Camilla a conventionally feminine desire for personal adornment. Commenting on lines 778–82, he paraphrases:

MAIDEN: . . . she follows the one (Chloreus), as though he were
alone on the field of battle in so great a throng of warriors. She was
doing this led on not by love of the youth but of his clothes . . .
blind from desire for the spoils of battle, seeing nothing beyond her
prey, which betrayed her to the lurking Arruns.   (2.529.17–26)

Interpreting the passage in the light of Roman cultural conventions concerning women's interests, cued by Virgil's *uirgo* (11.778) and *femineo*
(11.782), Donatus ascribes to Camilla the motivation of passionate
desire not for Chloreus but for his rich clothing, and he attributes her
fatal recklessness on the battlefield to her sex. A traditional Roman rhetoric of gender difference informs Donatus' interpretation of the passage
and is reinforced by his paraphrase.

With Camilla's fatal 'feminine' weakness for Chloreus' purple and gold
finery, we may compare Euryalus' disastrous decision to carry off the
spoils of his attack on the sleeping Rutulians. Nisus, realising that he and
Euryalus have engaged in excessive slaughter, calls a halt, and the two
friends prepare to leave the Rutulians' camp to carry out their mission to
Aeneas.

> multa uirum solido argento perfecta relinquunt
> armaque, craterasque simul, pulchrosque tapetas.
> Euryalus phaleras Rhamnetis et aurea bullis
> cingula, Tiburti Remulo ditissimus olim
> quae mittit dona, hospitio cum iungeret absens,
> Caedicus . . .
> haec rapit atque umeris nequiquam fortibus aptat.
> tum galeam Messapi habilem, cristisque decoram,
> induit. excedunt castris, et tuta capessunt.   (9.357–66)

They leave behind many men's weapons made of solid silver, many
drinking cups, and beautiful rugs. Euryalus snatches up Rhamnes'
boss and swordbelt with golden studs, gifts which once the fabulously
wealthy Caedicus sent to Remulus of Tibur pledging friendship
without a meeting . . . this Euryalus fits to his strong shoulders, but in
vain. Then he puts on Messapus' well-fitting helmet, embellished
with crests. They leave the camp, and make for safety.

Although Nisus and Euryalus forego the rich booty of the camp,
Euryalus despoils two Rutulian corpses, Rhamnes of his boss and gold-

studded sword-belt, Messapus of his spectacular crested helmet. Donatus comments approvingly on Euryalus' choice of spoils, and commends the youth for preferring the accoutrements of a warrior to the rich spoils of the Rutulians' camp: 'he despises what could be considered extraneous for the moment, and takes away that which adorns a brave man and can offer strength in the event of war' (2.236.28–237.1). Just as Donatus magnifies the feminine frivolity of Camilla's pursuit of Chloreus' effeminate battle-garb so he here exaggerates the strategic decision which prompts Euryalus to strip his slain enemies of their armour, the badge of masculinity in heroic epic, for he fails to note the deadly beauty which will fatally compromise the helmet's utility by betraying Euryalus to the enemy later in the book (9.373–4).[52]

In discussing these characters, Virgil's ancient commentators show a tendency to try to foreclose nuances of gender-construction that call into question Roman norms of gender difference. Thus although Virgil endows Camilla with masculine attributes (7.804–7), Donatus and Servius insistently scrutinise her femininity; and although Virgil includes feminine touches in his characterisation of Euryalus, especially in the image of fragile beauty which haunts his death (9.433–7), Donatus explores his heroic manliness. The commentators' apparent lack of interest in Virgil's creative transgressions of the norms of both gender and genre is especially conspicuous by comparison with the fascination his successors, notably Ovid and Statius, evince for the gender ambiguities of these figures.[53] Camilla, for example, is the primary model for Ovid's boar-hunting Atalanta (*Met.* 8.317–23), whom the Ovidian Meleager credits with the *uirtus* that eludes the rest of the (male) hunters (8.387), and for Statius' swift huntress (*Theb.* 4.267–8; 6.563–7); she is also an important model, along with Euryalus, for Statius' boy-hero Parthenopaeus ('Maiden-face'; cf. 4.336–7), who shares with his precursors both speed in the footrace (6.550–617; cf. *Aen.* 5.286–361, 7.806–11) and an androgynous beauty (9.691–703). The gulf between the commentary tradition

---

[52] Servius, by contrast, notes the poet's careful foreshadowing: 'he anticipates well when he says "embellished"; for Euryalus is taken when its brilliance gives him away'.

[53] Cf. Hinds (n.d.), 16, who wonders whether 'even elements which had been emplotted by Virgil as *transgressive* for epic . . . [could be] read [by subsequent epicists] as *normative* for the genre'. On the impact of the *Aeneid* on imperial epic, see Hardie (1993).

and the poetic tradition in this regard, as in so many others, bears out Horace's contemptuous contrast between the schoolmen and men of letters (S. 1.10.72–5).[54]

Modern scholarly discussion of Servius and Donatus, although often recognising the utility of their comments in enlarging our understanding of the poetry of Virgil's *Aeneid*, has aligned itself with Horace in deriding the literal-mindedness and perversity which the reading habits of the schoolmen reveal.[55] I would prefer to emphasise rather their typicality, but I must concede that we are severely hampered by the loss of so many ancient critical commentaries, particularly acute in the case of classical Latin epics other than the *Aeneid*.[56] The commentaries on Ennius' *Annales* mentioned by Suetonius are no longer extant; the grammatical notes of Verrius Flaccus on Lucretius' language and the critical edition of the *De rerum natura* by the Neronian scholar M. Valerius Probus have not survived; and there is no evidence that either Valerius Flaccus or Silius Italicus received commentaries in antiquity. Ovid's *Metamorphoses* and Lucan's *Bellum Ciuile*, while immensely popular throughout the imperial period, were never accorded a central place in the ancient curriculum, although they both seem to have received detailed commentary by late antiquity.[57] We are more fortunate still in the case of Statius, for the labours of at least one of his ancient commentators survive.

Statius' hope that his poem will endure depends in large part on its achievement of a place in the school curriculum. His hopes were fully realised: Juvenal is an early witness to the popularity of both poet and poem (Juv. 7.82–6), and the grammarians Servius and Priscian mention a commentary on Statius. A complete late fifth- or early sixth-century commentary on the *Thebaid* and *Achilleid*, attributed to Lactantius Placidus, survives.[58] Lactantius, like Servius, Donatus and the ancient commentators on Lucan, offers guidance in the interpretation of Statius' poetry that ranges from grammatical commentary to the citation of par-

---

[54] Cf. Hor. *Ep.* 1.20.17–18; Juv. 7.226–7.

[55] Kaster (1988), and Conte (1994), 627–9, are important exceptions.

[56] On Latin philology and the development of a Roman commentary tradition, see Kaster (1988), and Conte (1994), 571–87, 625–38.

[57] On the commentary tradition on Ovid's *Metamorphoses*, see Otis (1936), and Hollis (1996); the scholia to Lucan are collected in Endt (1969).

[58] Lactantius' commentaries were edited by Jahnke (1898).

allels from other authors (notably Virgil, Ovid and Lucan). Again like the ancient commentators on Virgil and Lucan, Lactantius regularly has recourse to ancient stereotypes of gender difference in his explication of the poem. He provides particularly focused comment in this vein in his analysis of the opening of Polyxo's speech to the Lemnian women early in *Thebaid* 5. Exhorting them to put aside the weakness of women, the aged Polyxo urges that they kill their husbands, who have abandoned them for Thracian concubines: *'Rem summam instinctu superum meritique doloris, | o uiduae (firmate animos et pellite sexum!) | Lemniades, sancire paro* ('"At the prompting of the gods and of just grief, o widowed women of Lemnos (take courage and banish your sex!), I undertake to sanction a matter of utmost urgency",' 5.104–6). Disturbed by Polyxo's injunction to the Lemnian women to act without regard for the limitations of their sex, Lactantius explains:

> SEX: he has not said 'forget your sex' (that is without alteration in respect to its nature, which could be changed in no way) but 'with your womanly weakness banished, assume manly courage for crime'.

Statius' commentator is at pains to make clear that these lines in no way call into question the 'natural' hierarchy of gender, explaining that the weakness characteristic of the female sex is innate and essential rather than socially constructed and regulated. Lactantius shares this assumption with the other commentators on Latin epic, who insistently document the essential differences that distinguish male from female and inform relations between the sexes. By schooling their students in the innate inferiority of woman to man, they reproduce and legitimate the social fact of male dominance in Roman antiquity.

Lactantius' assumptions about the essential nature of the female frequently resurface in his commentary on book five, in which Statius narrates the tale of the Lemnian women. Despite the women's easy victory over their husbands, they are defeated in a second battle between the sexes when they take up arms to resist the Argonauts' landing on the island of Lemnos. This is partially due to the intervention of Jupiter on the side of the Argonauts, for the god provokes a storm that causes the Lemnian women to panic: *diriguere animi, manibusque horrore remissis | arma aliena cadunt, rediit in pectora sexus* ('their courage turned, they dropped the alien weapons when their hands slackened from fright, and their sex returned to their breasts', 5.396–7). Again Lactantius offers invaluable assistance in interpreting the gender clichés that inform the passage:

> ALIEN WEAPONS he meant not the weapons belonging to their husbands, but weapons not their own, that is belonging to the other sex. For (she says) when through fear at the sight of the Argonauts we are summoned back to our sex, our (womanly) nature resumes its own (proper) strength, since it could not have attained in full a strength not our own.

For Lactantius, as for the commentators of Virgil and Lucan, weapons are not properly the province of the female sex. Even after the Lemnian women have used them to devastating effect against their husbands, weapons (*arma*, one of the two central topics of Virgilian and post-Virgilian epic) remain the prerogative of the epic male (*uir*) and his epigones, the (male) teachers and students of Roman epic.

Statius confirms at the outset of the *Thebaid* that he will follow the precedent of earlier Latin and Greek epicists and take as his focus men and arms, when he specifies 'fraternal slaughter' (*fraternas acies*, 1.1) as the subject of his poem. Like his predecessors, however, Statius frequently defines the male by reference to the female. Early in the *Thebaid*, the poet introduces Adrastus as the king of Argos and father of two daughters: *hic sexus melioris inops, sed prole uirebat | feminea, gemino natarum pignore fultus* ('he lacked children of the better sex, but was rich in female offspring, sustained by a twin surety of daughters', 1.393–4). This phrasing reflects the conventional superiority of male over female in ancient Roman society, and Lactantius implies that the sentiment is traditional in epic when he adduces in comparison Virgil's introduction of the Italian king Latinus (quoting *Aen.* 7.50–2).[59] Despite Statius' early assertion of the natural superiority of male over female, however, the final scenes of the *Thebaid* problematise the conventional epic opposition of women and *uirtus*. For after the defeat of the Argive forces at Thebes, one of Adrastus' daughters proposes that the Argive women brave the dangers of the battlefield to bury their dead husbands: *hic non femineae subitum uirtutis amorem | colligit Argia, sexuque inmane relicto | tractat opus* ('then Argia summoned up a sudden love of unwomanly courage,

---

[59] Cf. Lactantius' citation of *Aen.* 9.616 in reference to *Theb.* 9.795, quoted above n.39. For similar phrases, implying a hierarchy of the sexes, cf. *Theb.* 9.118, 609, 825–9.

and considered the huge task with no thought for her sex', 12.177–9). Lactantius has nothing to say about this passage, perhaps because it coheres so closely with his cultural biases; the lines implicitly confirm women's essential weakness, their distance from male standards of *uirtus*. Yet from another perspective, they seem to canvass the possibility that the female is fully capable of manly courage and to hint that female nature itself may not be fixed and immutable. This is a possibility the ancient commentators leave unexplored.

Epic poetry was supremely valorised as a literary form centred on the principle of elite male identity (*uirtus*) in the ancient Roman educational system, where the masculine focus of the genre was both mirrored and magnified. The ancient commentators articulate a traditional belief in the innate superiority of man over woman which they inculcate in their students. This assumption is often implicit in references to the female in Latin epic but it is elaborated in greater detail in the ancient commentaries, which contain our best evidence for the scholastic practices of reading epic in antiquity. Instruction in epic poetry played an early role in shaping the elite Roman male's understanding of the world he was socially destined to govern, and it naturalised and legitimated social hierarchies of class, nationality and gender. In this way, the ancient Roman educational system helped to provide the Roman elite with a practical justification of its own privilege.[60] While epic poetry and its commentators can tell us little about the self-perceptions of ancient Roman women, the poets' commentators reveal a great deal about the social expectations that shaped women's behaviour and justified their dominated status within Roman society.

---

[60] Cf. Habinek (1988). Bourdieu asserts (paraphrasing Marx and Engels [1932], 35) that 'the ruling ideas, in every age, [are] the ideas of the ruling class' and that 'the ruling ideas themselves reinforce the rule of that class': Bourdieu and Passeron (1977), vi; cf. 4–11, especially 9. On the survival of this androcentric culture of reading and the cultural prestige of imperial Rome, exemplified in the authority of the curricular authors, in medieval and renaissance Europe, see Curtius (1953), 58–61; Desmond (1994), 7–10; and Ong (1959), and (1962), 211–16.

CHAPTER

3

The ground of representation

> Restore to me the color of face
> And the warmth of body,
> The light of heart and eye,
> The salt of bread and earth . . . the Motherland.
> (M. Darwish, 'A Lover from Palestine')[1]

The metaphor that associates earth with the female body can be traced back to the archaic period of ancient Greece and beyond to the Vedic literature of ancient India.[2] Homer describes the earth as 'life-giving' (φυσίζοος αἶα, *Il.* 3.243; cf. 21.63, *Od.* 11.301), while Hesiod, in the *Theogony*, represents Gaia ('Earth') as the mother who initiates the generations of gods (126ff.) and men (571ff.).[3] Lucretius, Roman poet of Greek natural philosophy, succinctly articulates the connection in lines that establish an analogy between women's reproductive capacity and the seasonal fertility of the earth: *linquitur ut merito maternum nomen adepta | terra sit, e terra quoniam sunt cuncta creata* ('we conclude that the earth has deservedly won the name of mother, since all things are born of earth', 5.795–6; cf. 2.998, 5.821–5). Rarely, however, has the ground of the metaphor been as fully elaborated as it is in the simile Lucretius develops soon after.

---

[1] Quoted in Said (1993), 226.

[2] For anthropological discussion of the metaphor, see Ortner (1974) and Ardener (1975). For the metaphor in ancient Greece, see DuBois (1988), 39–85; Winkler (1990), 180–7; Jeffrey Henderson (1991), 135–6; and Dougherty (1993), 61–80; and in ancient Rome, see Adams (1982), 82–5.

[3] In the *Argonautica*, Apollonius rehearses the metaphor in the dream of the Argonaut Euphemus that a clod of earth is a maiden (4.1731–45): see Hunter (1993), 167–8.

tum tibi terra dedit primum mortalia saecla.
multus enim calor atque umor superabat in aruis.
hoc ubi quaeque loci regio opportuna dabatur,
crescebant uteri terram radicibus apti;
quos ubi tempore maturo patefecerat aetas
infantum fugiens umorem aurasque petessens,
conuertebat ibi natura foramina terrae
et sucum uenis cogebat fundere apertis
consimilem lactis, sicut nunc femina quaeque
cum peperit, dulci repletur lacte, quod omnis
impetus in mammas conuertitur ille alimenti.
terra cibum pueris, uestem uapor, herba cubile
praebebat . . .   (5.805–17)

Then the earth first gave forth living beings; for much heat and
moisture remained in the fields. Wherever there was a suitable
location, wombs grew up clinging to the earth by roots, and when
these, in due time, were laid open by the development of the infants
fleeing moisture and trying to reach the open air, nature turned in
their direction the apertures of the earth, and compelled a milk-like
juice to pour forth from her open veins, just as nowadays, each
woman, when she has given birth, is filled up with sweet milk, which
all the current of her nourishment turns towards her breasts. Earth
used to offer food for her children, warmth their clothing, and grass
a bed . . .

Lucretius employs the vocabulary of specifically human reproduction –
uterus and *mamma* with *infans*, *femina*, and *puer* – to describe the creation of animate life from the earth.[4] The passage thereby brings into focus
the paradox that human sexual difference, as the philosopher represents
it, is the result neither of human anatomy nor of the physiology of
human reproduction. On the contrary, the poet anthropomorphises
earth (and hot water) in philosophical discourse by treating sexual
difference as an *a priori* phenomenon.

This is not an isolated example: a propensity towards characterising

---

[4] Bailey (1947), 3.1457, notes that although 'these lines in general concern all animals
. . . and the human race is not specifically mentioned till 822, men are included in
mortalia saecla (805), and it is clear that in these lines Lucr. is thinking specially of
the human child'.

the earth as a generative female body is often noted in Lucretius. Georgia Nugent has recently argued, however, in a study of the representation of women in *De Rerum Natura*, that while Lucretius consistently feminises the earth, he also, conversely, reduces the female to insensate matter.[5] A passage in book two exemplifies his procedure.

> principio tellus habet in se corpora prima
> unde mare immensum uoluentes frigora fontes
> assidue renouent, habet ignes unde oriantur.
> . . .
> tum porro nitidas fruges arbustaque laeta
> gentibus humanis habet unde extollere possit,
> unde etiam fluuios frondis et pabula laeta
> montiuago generi possit praebere ferarum.
> quare magna deum mater materque ferarum
> et nostri genetrix haec dicta est corporis una.

$$(2.589\text{--}91, 594\text{--}9)$$

In the beginning, the earth holds within herself the primal bodies by which ocean's springs, whirling icy blasts, continuously renew the vast sea, [the primal bodies] by which fires arise . . . Then too she holds within the seeds from which she could produce the gleaming crops and fertile orchards for human peoples, and from which she could offer streams, leaves, and fruitful nourishment to the mountain-wandering race of beasts. Wherefore she alone is called the great mother of gods, the mother of beasts, and the mother of our body.

Lucretius illustrates the Epicurean argument that all matter is composed of more than one type of atom by appealing to the example of *Tellus* (Earth), whom he anthropomorphises as the great mother of gods, beasts and men. The repetition of *corpus* (2.589, 599), however, undermines the agency of mother earth by aligning the reproductive female body with corporeal substance: as Diskin Clay notes, '*et nostri genetrix* is radically modified by the word *corporis*. Even as it is introduced the conception of Mother Earth is reduced to matter.'[6] A favourite Lucretian wordplay deriving *mater*, 'mother', from *materies*, 'matter', and *terra*, 'earth',

<hr>

[5] Nugent (1994).   [6] Clay (1983), 229, quoted by Nugent (1994), 183.

underpins the movement here from mother to matter, generative body to insensate earth (cf. 2.652, *terra quidem uero caret omni tempore sensu*).[7]

The formulation *nostri genetrix corporis* is especially significant in this context because it recalls and supersedes the description of Venus in the opening words of the poem as the 'mother of Aeneas' descendants' (*Aeneadum genetrix*, 1.1).[8] In the course of the poem Lucretius strips from Venus the attributes applied to her in the proem and assigns them instead to 'the blind forces of inanimate nature',[9] so closely related (as Nugent shows) to 'the female, passive, insensate body . . . predicated of earth'.[10] Thus the poet applies the adjective *alma*, used of Venus in the proem (1.2), to *mater terra*, 'mother earth', in the following book (2.992–3), and already in book one he represents *natura*, rather than Venus or an anthropomorphised *mater terra*, as the 'source of things' (*rerum natura creatrix*, 1.629; cf. 1.227–9, 2.1117, 5.1362), the generative force which 'creates, increases and fosters all things' (*unde omnis natura creet res auctet alatque*, 1.56).[11] Lucretius thereby transforms the agency of a goddess or an anthropomorphic 'mother' earth into the passivity of inanimate matter.

Nugent's exploration of the depiction of women in *De Rerum Natura* leads her to conclude that Lucretius' portrait of a heroic Epicurus, laying bare nature's secrets by force (*sic natura tua ui | tam manifesta patens ex omni parte retecta est*, 3.29–30), invites interpretation as an illustration of the process whereby Lucretius constructs an active male subject through the subjugation of a passive female object (*terra, materies, mater, natura*). Of particular significance in this regard is the military imagery in which Epicurus' mastery of the secrets of nature (and concomitant conquest of superstition) is celebrated in the opening book:

> primum Graius homo . . .
> quem neque fama deum nec fulmina nec minitanti
> murmure compressit caelum, sed eo magis acrem
> irritat animi uirtutem, effringere ut arta

---

[7] On Lucretius' punning complex *mater-materies-terra*, see Nugent (1994), 182–6, with bibliography. On the association of woman with dirt in Roman culture generally, see Richlin (1984) and (1992c), 113–16; the classic statement of the connection in anthropology is Douglas (1966).

[8] Clay (1983), 82–110, 226–32; and Gale (1994), 208–28, with further bibliography.

[9] Gale (1994), 212.   [10] Nugent (1994), 186.   [11] Cf. 1.262–4, 2.224, 879–80.

> naturae primus portarum claustra cupiret.
> ergo uiuida uis animi peruicit, et extra
> processit longe flammantia moenia mundi
> atque omne immensum peragrauit mente animoque,
> unde refert nobis uictor quid possit oriri,
> quid nequeat, finita potestas denique cuique
> quanam sit ratione atque alte terminus haerens.   (1.66–77)

First a Greek man . . . whom neither report of the gods nor thunderbolts nor heaven's menacing murmur checked, but provoked his spirit's courage the more keenly, so that he desired to be the first to break the narrow bolts of the gates of nature. Then the lively force of his mind prevailed, and he proceeded far beyond the flaming walls of the world and travelled in mind and spirit through the immense whole, whence the conqueror reports to us what can come into existence, what cannot, in sum by what form of rational explanation each thing's power is limited and the boundary-stone sticks fast.

Through the application of epic themes and military imagery to Epicurus' discovery of the laws of nature, the poet represents the Greek philosopher as a victorious Roman general who has conquered superstition by mastering nature.[12] The reference to Epicurus' breach of the portals of nature (1.70–1) draws on a conventional epic analogy between the sexual penetration of a woman's body and the conquest of enemy territory to which the Homeric Achilles appeals in the *Iliad* in his prayer that he and Patroclus 'alone may breach Troy's holy corona' (*Il.* 16.100). Through Lucretius' military metaphor, Epicurus achieves the heroic conquest of a feminised ground of resistance that had eluded the paradigmatic Homeric hero. The poet also implicitly portrays Epicurus' success as a Roman triumph (*quare religio pedibus subiecta uicissim | obteritur, nos exaequat uictoria caelo*, 1.78–9), a victory parade in which were displayed images of the conquered enemy represented allegorically in the form of female personifications.[13] Lucretius thus depicts the Epicurean claim to universal knowledge in terms of spatial conquest.

In addition to deploying epic and military codes of imagery in this passage, Lucretius engages the contemporary cartographic discourse of

---

[12] Gale (1994), 118.   [13] Toynbee (1934), 7–23; Ostrowski (1996).

Roman imperialism to map Epicurus' conquest of the secrets of nature. In the late Republic, Roman power comes to be represented as coterminous with the known world.[14] Thus Pompey claims to have brought 'the boundaries of the empire to the limits of the earth' (Diod. Sic. 40.4) and Cicero defines the limits of Roman authority as coextensive with the world (*Sest.* 67). Just as Rome under Pompey and Julius Caesar decisively establishes her domination over the whole of the world, so Epicurus here surveys the whole of nature and establishes man's dominion over her by publishing a 'map' of nature that will free us from superstition. Although Lucretius explicitly identifies nature as the source and limit of all things, the rhetoric in which the passage is couched implicitly transforms Epicurus' knowledge of nature's *termini* into a mastery of nature: his report of what nature can and cannot do, of her extent and boundaries, constitutes a 'map' of nature that reduces her from the engine of all creation to the object of man's control. Lucretius thereby represents the Epicurean organisation of nature, which constitutes the subject of his poem 'On the Nature of the World', as analogous to contemporary Roman organisation of empire. The Epicurean world Lucretius depicts reflects the interpenetration of Greek philosophical and Roman social hierarchies of order, including the subordination of nature to philosopher, *orbis terrarum* ('the inhabited world') to Rome, and woman to man.

In this chapter we shall explore the complex interrelations linking male mastery of a feminised landscape in Latin epic with political and social constructions of Roman order. Recent discussion of the concepts of nature and landscape among geographers, art historians, and literary critics, has emphasised that they are cultural images and not empirical objects.[15] Commentary on the European 'discourse of discovery' about the 'New World', for example, has implicated the Tudor vocabulary of sexual difference in colonial strategies of political domination and economic profit. Patricia Parker draws attention to the political and economic motives that link 'the organization and laying out of land with other forms of order' in European descriptions of the Americas.[16] In a passage of considerable interest to us, she invokes Virgil's *Aeneid* as an exemplary text in mapping North America:

---

[14] See Nicolet (1991), *passim*, and especially 31–56, with bibliography.
[15] Rose (1993), 89, with further bibliography. See also Kolodny (1975); Parker (1987), 126–54; Montrose (1991); and Cheyfitz (1997), 70–2.   [16] Parker (1987), 151.

the impulse in such writings . . . to bring something under the control of the eye or gaze calls to mind not just Virgil's *Georgics* but also his *Aeneid*, the epic of empire self-consciously present for so many of the 'diligent writers' of the New World. Both its cartographic impulse and its repeated topos of taking command from a high place might suggest why imperial gaze and male gaze come together so readily in the New World texts, where the impulse to master or dominate a feminized landscape is at the same time a matter for the eye.[17]

Latin epic as a genre is centrally concerned with Roman mastery of the (Mediterranean) world from the outset: the theme repeatedly arises not only in the avowedly historical epics, but also, as we have seen, in Lucretius' philosophical poem; even Ovid and Valerius Flaccus engage the genre's imperialist impulse in the deployment of the topos of *translatio imperii* at programmatic moments in their mythological epics.[18] I shall argue that the gender asymmetry of Roman social relations is both constituted and expressed through the spatial organisation of epic. Let us begin, therefore, at the beginning – of Rome and Roman epic – with the rape of Ilia in Ennius' *Annales*.

Our knowledge of Ennius' treatment of the rape of Ilia is almost entirely derived from Cicero's quotation, in *de Divinatione* (1.40–1), of a dream reported by Ilia to her half-sister, the daughter of Aeneas' first wife Eurydica (*Eurydica prognata*, 36).[19] Cicero begins his quotation of the Ennian passage with the arrival of an old woman, probably a nurse, carrying a light (*et cita cum tremulis anus attulit artubus lumen*, 34). The setting of Ilia's report of the dream that has just disturbed her sleep (*talia tum memorat lacrimans, exterrita somno*, 35) is generally agreed to be her bedroom, but the context in which the passage is preserved precludes certainty. Ennius seems to locate Ilia in an interior domestic setting removed from public ground or civic space, despite her status as a Vestal Virgin.[20] This setting is strongly marked as a female space by the presence of the aged attendant and Ilia's half-sister. By contrast, Ilia encounters in her dream two shadowy male figures, Mars and Aeneas. Mars appears as the handsome man who drags her along the banks of a river (*nam me uisus*

---

[17] Parker (1987), 151.   [18] Ov. *Met.*1.3–4, 15.622–879; V.Fl. 1.531–60.

[19] I cite the fragments of Ennius' *Annales* from Skutsch (1985).

[20] Cicero implies that Ennius cast her as a Vestal: see Skutsch (1985), 195–6.

homo pulcer per amoena salicta | et ripas raptare locosque nouos, 38–9), before disappearing from the landscape in which she represents herself as wandering alone (*ita sola | postilla, germana soror, errare uidebar*, 39–40). She looks for her sister (*tardaque uestigare et quaerere te neque posse | corde capessere*, 41–2), but it is her father Aeneas who responds to her cries with words of comfort (*exim compellare pater me uoce uidetur | his uerbis*, 43–4).

The metaphor of sexual initiation in the poet's reference to the unfamiliar landscape in which Ilia finds herself (*locos nouos*, 39) alerts us to the sexual symbolism implicit in the spatial organisation of the passage as a whole.[21] Ennius' portrayal of Ilia dreaming about her rape in her bedroom evokes chaste and inviolable Homeric princesses dreaming of marriage in their bedrooms.[22] The debt to Homer's portrait of Nausicaa is especially strongly marked, for Ennius has conflated the successive scenes of Nausicaa's dream in her bedroom and subsequent erotic encounter by the river with a seductive stranger, Odysseus, into the single scene of Ilia in her bedroom dreaming about an encounter with a handsome stranger, Mars, amid pleasant willow thickets by the banks of a river. In his description of the dreamscape in which Ilia is ravished, Ennius draws on a long tradition of vegetation and water metaphors that inscribe a topography of the female sexual organs in the *locus amoenus* landscape.[23] The 'metaphor of the field, garden, meadow, etc. applied to the female pudenda',[24] is frequently developed in Latin literature, both alone and in conjunction with the 'virginal associations of the fresh water of rivers or pools'[25] which Latin poets derived from Greek literature. The setting of Ilia's dream hints further at latent sexual violence, for in his account of her rape Ennius also alludes to Homer's treatment of the rape of Tyro by Poseidon at the bank of the river Enipeus (*Od.* 11.235–59).[26]

---

[21] Connors (1994) 108 n.25.
[22] See Krevans (1993), 262–3, on Ennius' allusions to Nausicaa and Penelope, both on the verge of an erotic encounter with Odysseus. On sexual metaphors in houshold terminology and in references to doors, see Adams (1982), 86–9, and Jeffrey Henderson (1991), 137–8.
[23] On this imagery, see Parry (1957); Parry (1964); Segal (1969); Adams (1982); DuBois (1988); Winkler (1990), 180–2; and Jeffrey Henderson (1991).
[24] Adams (1982), 82–3.   [25] Segal (1969), 24.
[26] Skutsch (1985), 194: cf. Dominik (1993), 42; Krevans (1993), 264; and Connors (1994) 102–5. On the connotation of sexual violence in *raptare*, see Adams (1982), 175.

The setting of Ilia's rape in the *Annales* thus oscillates between an interior domestic space and an as-yet undefined territory out of doors beyond the limits of Amulius' kingdom. The poet locates Ilia both within the *domus* and at the same time beyond the bounds of civic space altogether, in 'unknown places'. The new places of Ilia's dream have further symbolic resonance in that they prefigure the foundation of Rome.[27] In her dream Ilia wanders a pathless landscape that lacks the characteristic signs of human frequentation (*semita nulla pedem stabilibat*, 42), but this primeval unmarked landscape will be defined and demarcated as a city by one of the sons conceived in this rape. Mars' sexual conquest of Ilia thus prefigures her son's political mastery of this very landscape: both Ilia and the primordial landscape are sites to be possessed and defined by male political agents. Moreover Ennius finally fixes Ilia herself permanently in the primeval landscape that will be brought under political control – objectified and defined by the *pomerium* – when, on Amulius' command, his 'hired warriors' toss her into the river (*haec ecfatus, ibique latrones dicta facessunt*, 57; cf. fr. xxxix). In the logic of Ennius' narrative, the site of the future city of Rome, itself the dreamscape of Ilia's sexual initiation, is the site of her death.

The surviving fragments do not disclose Amulius' motive for drowning Ilia in the river, but her persecution at his hands is conventionally interpreted in the light of later Roman treatments of her story.[28] Livy, Horace and Ovid apparently follow Ennius in their characterisation of the twins' mother as a Vestal Virgin *avant la lettre*, whose sacralised chastity is imposed upon her by the usurper Amulius out of a desire to oust Aeneas' descendants from the throne, and who is punished with death for *incestum*, 'unchastity', after the rape.[29] Her representation as a Vestal is further facilitated by the similarities between her death and the penalty traditionally meted out to unchaste Vestals.[30] Punished for 'her' sexual transgression by being thrown alive into the river, Ilia anticipates the fate

---

[27] See Krevans (1993), on the connection between 'seduction' dreams and city-foundation myths.

[28] Liv. 1.3.4–5; Hor. *Carm.* 1.2.13–20; Ov. *Fast.* 3.11–58, and *Am.* 3.6.45–82; cf. Dion. Hal. *Ant. Rom.* 1.76–8, Plu. *Rom.* 3.2–3. See further Bremmer and Horsfall (1987), 27–30, on Ilia in the mythographic tradition.

[29] Skutsch (1985), 195–6, 212–13; Beard (1989), 47.

[30] On Vestals put to death for *incestum*, see Fraschetti (1984); on the ancients' preoccupation with the Vestals' transgression of their vow of chastity, see Beard (1995), 171–3.

of historical Vestal Virgins condemned for *incestum* and interred alive at the Colline Gate.

Paradoxically, however, the setting of Ilia's death is the scene of life-giving rescue for her sons Romulus and Remus, whose exposure on the river follows closely upon her immersion in it (65–8). The twins are spared when they wash up on the river bank beneath a fruit tree laden with 'sweet figs dripping milk from the whole breast' (*fici dulciferae lactantes ubere toto, sed. inc.* fr. vi).[31] The proto-Roman landscape, which closely resembles the dreamscape *locus amoenus* of Ilia's rape, assumes the lost mother's role as nurturer. Ennius thus seems to have fostered a symbolic connection between the immersion of Ilia in the Tiber and the maternal sustenance of the pre-political landscape that rescues her sons. In this regard, Ilia's union with the Tiber – whether through death by drowning or 'marriage' to the river god – bears a suggestive resemblance to foundation sacrifice.[32] Just as the murder of Remus at the hands of his brother Romulus after leaping the newly-founded city's walls guarantees the impregnability of the city, so Ilia's union with the river guarantees her sons' lives at the river-bank on the site where Romulus will found Rome.[33]

In associating the site of Ilia's rape and death so closely with the future site of Rome, Ennius combines several themes prominent in the Greek epic tradition, including the heroic genealogy and the *ktisis* or 'foundation' narrative.[34] Ennius also borrows from Greek literature the traditional metaphor that tropes the female sexual organs in the *locus amoenus*.[35] However he literalises the Greek metaphor by locating a specific woman in the idealised landscape of primeval Rome. The city's founder is born of a woman whose erotic potential is symbolically mirrored in the dreamscape setting of her rape, while the maternal succour of the site of Rome symbolically arises from her immersion in that setting. The site of Rome is thus coded as successively a sexual and a

---

[31] Skutsch (1985), 605–6, acknowledges that the line is likely to come from book one; cf. Liv. 1.4.5, on the *ficus Ruminalis*.

[32] On foundation sacrifice (*Bauopfer*), see Sartori (1898). For Ilia's death as marriage with the river, see chapter five, pp. 105–6.

[33] Prop. 3.9.50; cf. Flor. *Epit.* 1.1.8. On Remus' death as a foundation sacrifice, see Wiseman (1995), 124–6. For a different interpretation of 'founding violence' in the story of Ilia, see Joplin (1990), 58–9.

[34] Bremmer-Horsfall (1987), 27–30; Krevans (1993).

[35] Cf. DuBois (1988), 63. On the metaphor in Greek myths of colonisation, see Dougherty (1993), 61–80.

maternal landscape, and the ground of that encoding is Ilia's successively virginal and maternal body. Ilia's submersion in the pre-political landscape of Rome endows the site of the proto-Roman state with maternal substance even as it erases a specific mother from Roman history and culture.

Ennius' association of the primeval landscape of Rome with the reproductive body of Ilia anticipates the emergence in the triumviral period of an overlap in the iconographies of *Tellus* ('mother Earth') and Italy.[36] In the *Georgics*, for example, Virgil identifies *Tellus* with the 'Saturnian land' (Italy), which he hails as the 'great mother of crops and men' (*salue, magna parens frugum, Saturnia tellus, | magna uirum*, 2.173–4). In the *Aeneid*, Virgil extends this association in his treatment of a myth of Rome's origins which similarly conjoins the maternal body with the Italian landscape. The opening lines of the poem announce the hero's mission in words that set in play a foundation narrative (1.1–7).[37] The goal of Aeneas' journey is Italy, particularised as Latium in the phrase 'Lavinian shores' (*Lauiniaque . . . litora*, 1.1–2) where tradition located Lavinium, Aeneas' first foundation in Italy. Aeneas is characterised as an *oikist*, 'founding hero', throughout the poem and particlarly in book three where he unsuccessfully founds two cities, one in Thrace (3.16–18) and a second in Crete (3.132–4). After the first failed foundation in Thrace, Aeneas consults the oracle of the god Apollo in his temple on Delos and is told to return to 'the first land which bore Dardan stock', the Trojans' 'ancient mother' ('*Dardanidae duri, quae uos a stirpe parentum | prima tulit tellus, eadem uos ubere laeto | accipiet reduces. antiquam exquirite matrem*', 3.94–6). In these lines, Virgil redescribes territorial conquest in Italy as a return to the maternal body.

The metaphor of the maternal landscape is particularly strongly drawn in the phrase *ubere laeto* (3.95), 'with fruitful breast', an adaptation of the Homeric οὖθαρ ἀρούρης ('the earth's udder', *Il.* 9.141, 283), a traditional metaphor for fertility, conventionally translated 'the richest, most fertile land'. On Virgil's phrase Servius comments: '*uber*, "teat, pap" is strictly speaking *fecunditas*, "fruitfulness, fertility"'.[38] His slide to metaphor, often echoed by modern critics, is instructive in its elision of woman from

---

[36] Zanker (1988), 172–83; Galinsky (1996), 106–21.

[37] Cf. *Aen.* 1.33. On *ktisis* narratives in the *Aeneid*, see Horsfall (1989), and Krevans (1993), 268–71.

[38] On *Aen.* 1.531, *ubere glaebae*; cf. *Aen.* 3.164.

epic: *uber* does not refer to the breast but rather to a metaphorical fertil-ity and abundance of the natural landscape of Italy. Even if we cannot be literal readers, however, we can press the metaphor further. Throughout the *Aeneid*, antiquity and fecundity are the hallmarks not so much of the characters who are mothers – Venus is an obvious example – but of primeval Italy. Aeneas echoes Apollo's description of the gener-ative potential of the Italian landscape when he tells Dido that the Trojans' destination is an ancient land of wonderful fertility and mighty warriors (*terra antiqua, potens armis atque ubere glaebae*, 1.531). In book 3, the portent of the white sow with thirty piglets is revealed to Aeneas by Helenus as the sign that Aeneas will have reached the end of his labours and the site of his city: *ingens inuenta sub ilicibus sus | triginta capitum fetus enixa iacebit, | alba solo recubans, albi circum ubera nati, | is locus urbis erit, requies ea certa laborum* ('you will find a great white sow, new mother of thirty piglets, lying beneath ilex trees and spreading her flank on the ground, her white offspring round her teats; that will be the site of your city, sure respite of your labours', 3.390–3). The sow's fecun-dity embodies the wonderful fertility of Italy in a symbolic conjunction of mother with the ground of the state that recalls both the maternal sus-tenance of the fig-tree on the site of primeval Rome and the she-wolf that suckles Ilia's twins in the *Annales.*

We may press the maternal metaphor of the oracle of Delos still further into the detail of the text in connection with the site that marks the arrival of the Trojans in Latium. The town and promontory of Caieta are situated on the borders of Latium and Campania, so that it is only with Aeneas' arrival at Port Caieta in the closing lines of book 6, and not with his arrival on the 'Euboean' shores of Cumae at the opening of the book (6.2), that Aeneas reaches his destination of Latium: *tum se ad Caietae recto fert limite portum. | ancora de prora iacitur; stant litore puppes* ('then they sail on a direct path to the port of Caieta and drop anchor; the ships stand on the shore', 6.900–1). The opening of the fol-lowing book attributes the name of the harbour to the death there of Aeneas' nurse, Caieta: *tu quoque litoribus nostris, Aeneia nutrix, | aeter-nam moriens famam, Caieta, dedisti* ('you too Caieta, nurse of Aeneas, gave everlasting fame to our shores by dying', 7.1–2). The phrase *Aeneia nutrix* resonates symbolically with Apollo's characterisation of the land the Trojans are to settle as *ubere laeto . . . antiquam matrem* (3.95–6): Caieta embodies the *antiquam matrem* to whom Aeneas is instructed to

return. Her death on and burial in Italian soil at this juncture symbolically confirm the successful return of the Trojans to their ancient homeland in Italy, and this symbolism underwrites her corporeal assimilation
into the physical features of the terrain of primeval Latium. Her dignity
is preserved in the territory (*nunc seruat honos sedem tuus*, 7.3) while her
name marks the location of her bones in Italy (*ossaque nomen | Hesperia
in magna, si qua est ea gloria, signat*, 7.3–4), in a passage that precisely
enacts the metaphor of inscription (Parker's 'cartographic impulse').

The death of Aeneas' nurse is commonly viewed as the third and final
death in a sequence of 'sacrificial' deaths of Aeneas' adherents, initiated
by Palinurus (6.347–84) and Misenus (6.162–74), that secure the Trojans'
safe 'return' to their original homeland, Italy.[39] Certainly Palinurus dies
explicitly to ensure the safe arrival of the Trojans in Italy (5.812–15) and
Misenus implicitly to secure Aeneas' safe passage through the underworld (6.149–55, on the model of Elpenor's death in the *Odyssey*).[40]
Caieta's death on the shore of Latium, however, participates in no such
sequence of structured exchange. Moreover her death on land
differentiates her from Palinurus and Misenus who both die in the sea just
off the Italian shore (6.350–62; 6.171–4). The men's sacrificial deaths
therefore seem better interpreted as testimony to the dangers of the
arduous sea voyage to Italy and the hazards entailed in the survivors'
journey from Troy. Commemoration of their deaths dramatises the slow
and difficult progress of the Trojans towards their goal, as well as the hostility of both Italians and gods to that goal. The death of Caieta operates
in a different symbolic register: her death commemorates the Trojans'
successful arrival in Latium, just as the assimilation of her body to the
ground of Italy prefigures her compatriots' assimilation to Latin stock
through political alliance and intermarriage.

When the Trojans leave Port Caieta and sail along the coast of Latium,
Virgil lingers over their progress past 'the shores of Circe's land' (*proxima
Circaeae raduntur litora terrae*, 7.10), in a figure that also feminises the
ground of primeval Italy, but to rather different effect. Circe's home has

[39] Lee (1979), 68–9; Putnam (1995), 103. On 'sacrificial crisis' in the *Aeneid* and later
epic, see Hardie (1993), 19–56; on the death of Palinurus in *Aeneid* 5, see Nugent
(1992), 284–8.

[40] *Od.* 10.551–60, 11.51–80. On ritual substitution in the deaths of Palinurus and
Misenus, see Otis (1963), 280–1; Lee (1979), 61–2; on the 'strongly utilitarian social
conscience' implicit in this structure, see Nugent (1992), 274–8.

'a fascinatingly tangential relationship'[41] to the Italian mainland: an island in book 3 (*Aeaeaeque insula Circae*, 3.386) following Homer (*Od.* 10.135), it is not obviously an island here (although *Circaeae . . . terrae* punningly alludes to the Homeric name of her island, Aeaea),[42] and at the end of the book it is a promontory (*Circaeum iugum*, 7.799). Circe invests her territory not with maternal plenitude but with seductive charm and menace. Her 'unapproachable' glades, glimpsed from afar in the night, hold out the promise of manifold sensual pleasures, for they are redolent with the scent of the cedar torches which light her weaving as she sings (7.11–14). But Virgil adds an undertone of menace to the sensual seductiveness of Circe's grove in the howls of rage uttered by the beasts, once men, who surround her home (7.15–20). The metamorphoses of her landscape reflect the witch's traditional powers of transformation, which the Trojans are spared. Neptune speeds the Trojans' ships past Circe's 'dread shores' (*litora dira*, 7.22) as a reward for their piety (7.21–4; cf. *pius Aeneas*, 7.5). Circe's territory offers no comforting maternal breast to the Trojan survivors, but a landscape that hints at the dangerous pleasures of female sexuality.[43]

The shifting associations of the feminised landscape of *magna Hesperia* culminate in the inscription of Lavinia, Latinus' daughter and only surviving child, in her father's territory of Latium. The key to both the future of Latinus' royal line and the success of Aeneas' epic *labores*, Lavinia 'alone remained in Latinus' house and preserved so great an estate' (*sola domum et tantas seruabat filia sedes*, 7.52). Although Lavinia is located at the centre of her father's household (*domus*), she defines the extent of her father's territory (*sedes*) in Latium, so that she too is in some sense constitutive of the topography of Italy. In response to the Trojans' request for a small territory in Latinus' kingdom (*sedem exiguam*, 7.229), Latinus pledges the fertility of his land (*non uobis rege Latino | diuitis uber agri Troiaeue opulentia deerit*, 'while Latinus is king, you will not miss the fertility (literally 'breast') of a rich land nor the wealth of Troy', 7.261–2) and promises his daughter Lavinia to Aeneas in marriage (7.268–73). The political foundation of Lavinium, which lies beyond the narrative scope of the *Aeneid* itself, is predicated within the poem on a dynastic marriage with Lavinia, and her sexual maturity – she is 'ripe for a husband' (*matura*

[41] Denis Feeney, *per litteras.*   [42] Stephen Hinds, *per litteras.*
[43] For Circe's tellurian associations here, see Segal (1968).

uiro, 7.53), in another agricultural metaphor – guarantees the fertility of the ground of the state (*diuitis uber agri*, 7.262). The opening lines of the poem define Aeneas' goal in Italy as 'Lavinian shores', in a phrase that collapses the twin political goals of marriage alliance and city foundation into one. Although Lavinia herself never speaks in the *Aeneid*, the city of Lavinium (12.194), traditionally the home of the very Penates which Hector entrusts to Aeneas (2.293–5) and the goal of Aeneas' journey, the *telos* of his epic *labores* (1.1–3), will take its name from her.[44] Lavinium in the *Aeneid* is an idealised site founded on political marriage with Lavinia, 'a representation of' Lavinia, as Lavinia is 'the ground of that representation'.[45]

In the *Metamorphoses*, Ovid carefully reproduces Virgil's specification of the destination of Aeneas and the Trojans as 'an ancient mother' (*antiquam matrem*, 13.678), and he maintains the connection between the arrival of the Trojans in Latium proper with the death and burial of Caieta (14.441–50).[46] The inscription of Caieta, among others,[47] in primeval Italy at the end of the *Metamorphoses* is predicated on the reuse of the Lucretian metaphor of *Tellus*, 'mother Earth', in the opening books of the epic where Ovid undertakes to narrate the origins of the cosmos.[48] Of course this can be no easy task in a poem which takes transformation as its subject: the cosmic order of the *Metamorphoses* is repeatedly threatened with the dissolution of the boundaries that separate land from sky (1.5–20, 151–5), sea (1.253–61, 274–5, 291–2, 313–15) and fiery upper air (2.272–300). With each successive re-establishment of the cosmic order, however, the earth is the more firmly secured as the stable site of others' transformation. The metaphorical association of the earth with

---

[44] Cf. Oliensis (1997), 307.

[45] De Lauretis (1984), 12, discussing the fictional city of Zobeide in Italo Calvino's *Invisible Cities*. She appropriates the phrase 'ground of representation' from the semiotics of C.S. Peirce, who defines the 'sign, or representamen, [as] something which stands to somebody . . . for something, its *object*. It stands for that object, not in all respects, but in reference to a sort of idea, which I have sometimes called the *ground* of the representation' (Peirce (1931), II.228, quoted in De Lauretis (1987), 39).

[46] Cf. Myers (1994), 104, on Ovid's astute 'correction' at *Met.* 14.157 of Virgil's anachronistic ascription of the name Caieta to the promontory (6.900), before her death (7.1–5).

[47] Cf. Pomona (*Met.* 14.622–771), on whom see Myers (1994a), 229, and Gentilcore (1995).   [48] *Met.* 1.80–8, 156–60, 383–413, 416–40; 3.102–25; 7.121–42.

the maternal body is clearly formulated in the aftermath of the great flood that Jupiter sends to purge the earth of the iniquitous generation of Lycaon (1.240–3). Only one man and one woman survive, and while Jupiter restores the cosmos (1.328–48), it falls to Deucalion and Pyrrha to regenerate humankind (1.363–6, 377–83). They consult the oracle of Themis and are told to repair the loss by throwing the bones of their great mother behind them (*ossaque post tergum magnae iactate parentis*, 1.383). Themis' oracle recalls that of Apollo (who will succeed her at Delphi, 1.443–51) in the *Aeneid* instructing Aeneas to seek the *antiquam matrem* of the Dardan race (3.94–6), and Deucalion correctly interprets his aged parent as the earth, her bones as rocks (*magna parens terra est: lapides in corpore terrae | ossa reor dici*, 1.393–4). The earth herself then regenerates the animal kingdom (1.416–21, 434–7), with such success that Jupiter can later explain his possession of an extremely attractive cow, the unfortunate Io, as a result of the wonderful fecundity of the earth (*Iuppiter e terra genitam mentitur*, 1.615).[49]

A final challenge to the stability of the epic order of the poem arises from the conflagration ignited by Phaethon's reckless driving of the Sun's chariot. Unable to endure the heat, *Tellus* intervenes to rescue the cosmos from flames:

> alma tamen Tellus, ut erat circumdata ponto,
> inter aquas pelagi contractosque undique fontes,
> qui se condiderant in opacae uiscera matris,
> sustulit oppressos collo tenus arida uultus
> opposuitque manum fronti magnoque tremore
> omnia concutiens paulum subsedit et infra,
> quam solet esse, fuit fractaque ita uoce locuta est   (2.272–8)

Nevertheless, kindly mother Earth, just as she was, surrounded by the sea, amid the waters of ocean and, retreating on every side, rivers, which had hidden themselves in the entrails of their dark mother, parched (from the fires) raised her smothered face as far as the neck; she placed a hand to her forehead, and striking the world with a mighty shaking, she sank down a bit below her usual place, and spoke with cracked voice.

---

[49] On the cosmogonic resonances in Ovid's use of the figure of 'mother Earth' in the *Metamorphoses*, see Myers (1994), 43–7.

Ovid here deploys imagery drawn from human anatomy (*collo, uultus, manum fronti, uoce*) and specifically female reproductive anatomy (*uiscera matris*) to map the physical features of an anthropomorphic mother Earth. The Earth herself characterises the effect of the flames on her 'body' in a speech that further delineates the interrelation between earth and woman: *'uix equidem fauces haec ipsa in uerba resoluo';* | *(presserat ora uapor) 'tostos en adspice crines* | *inque oculis tantum, tantum super ora fauillae!'* ('"indeed I can scarcely open my throat for these words" (the steam had choked her mouth); "just look at my burnt hair, and the ashes in my eyes and on my face!"', 2.282–4). This is the lengthiest intervention of *Tellus* in the poem (2.272–300), but it is also her last, for she is finally, immutably, fixed as the matrix of the world of the *Metamorphoses* at the conclusion of her speech: *suumque* | *rettulit os in se propioraque manibus antra* ('she hid her face deep within her caves next to the underworld', 2.302–3).

In response to the plea of the prostrate and helpless mother Earth, Jupiter 'the all-powerful father' (*pater omnipotens*) ascends to heaven's heights (from which he routinely surveys the earth below), to put an end to the fires (2.304–8). It is likewise Jupiter 'the all-powerful father' (*pater omnipotens*, 2.401), and not mother Earth, who restores the ground of the narrative in the aftermath of Phaethon's death. After surveying the foundations of the cosmos in order to discover and repair any damage (2.401–4), Jupiter examines the newly insensate earth and replenishes her rivers, grass and forests while on a tour of inspection in Arcadia (2.405–8). The passage details a stark contrast between the inert passivity of 'mother' earth and the omnipotent activity of 'father' Jupiter, whose circuit of exploration articulates the close connection between male domination of the feminised earth and the 'impulse . . . to bring something under the control of the eye or gaze'.[50]

By contrast to the many feminised landscapes of the *Metamorphoses*, Lucan's *Bellum Ciuile* includes only one fully elaborated example of the metaphorical association of earth with the female body. As Caesar's general Curio prepares to bring the Roman civil war to Africa in book four of the poem, Lucan postpones the battle narrative with a brief

---

[50] Ovid explores the interconnections linking control of the gaze with male power and the feminisation of landscape more fully in the tale of Hermaphroditus and Salmacis (4.285–388): see Keith (1999).

account of a mythological contest, Hercules' defeat of the Libyan giant Antaeus (4.593–660), that alludes extensively to Virgil's contest between Hercules and the monster Cacus on the site of primeval Rome (*Aen.* 8.184–275).[51] The introduction to the contest takes the form of a birth narrative in which the Libyan earth embodies the role of the Virgilian *antiqua mater* or the Ovidian *magna parens*: *nondum post genitos Tellus ecfeta gigantas | terribilem Libycis partum concepit in antris* ('mother Earth, after she had borne the giants, was not yet past child-bearing; she conceived a monstrous child in the Libyan caves', 4.593–4). Lucan portrays *Tellus*, 'mother Earth', in such a way as to evoke the traditional maternal fecundity of the primeval epic landscape, frequently, although not exclusively, Italian in earlier Latin epic: *nec tam iusta fuit Terrarum gloria Typhon | aut Tityos Briareusque ferox; caeloque pepercit | quod non Phlegraeis Antaeum sustulit aruis* ('not so deserving was Earth's fame for her sons Typhon, Tityos or savage Briareus; she spared heaven because she did not bear Antaeus in the Phlegraean Fields', 4.595–7). The portrait of Earth as Antaeus' mother and nurse is consonant with Virgil's depiction of Latium as an old mother metaphorically rich in milk, especially in view of the reference to Earth nurturing her son in the Libyan desert (4.594) rather than in Italian fields (4.597). This birth narrative also recalls the Lucretian account of the creation of life from a maternal landscape (5.805–17), but Lucan's mother Earth remains a source of succour and plenitude for her last child even after his birth: *hoc quoque tam uastas cumulauit munere uires | Terra sui fetus, quod cum tetigere parentem, | iam defecta uigent renouato robore membra* ('with this gift too, mother Earth endowed her son's great strength, whereby when his limbs touched his mother, though already failing, they grew vigorous with renewed force', 4.598–600). Throughout the episode, Lucan exploits the double significance of *Terra* and *Tellus* as both 'ground' and 'mother Earth'.[52]

Antaeus wreaks havoc on the local population until Hercules, in the course of ridding the earth of monsters (*terras . . . aequorque leuantem*, 4.610, an allusion to the Virgilian model), is drawn to Libya by Antaeus'

---

[51] Ahl (1976), 91–9.

[52] Cf. Martindale (1981), 73. Silius Italicus lays bare Lucan's play with the metaphor in a meticulously literal exposition of Antaeus' relation to *Tellus*: *nec leuior uinci Libycae telluris alumnus | matre super* ('nor was the child of the Libyan earth, standing on his mother, an easier conquest', Sil. 3.40–1).

evil reputation. Lucan's two mythological heroes prepare for quasi-gladiatorial combat:[53] Hercules greases himself up with olive oil following the conventions of the Olympic games (*perfudit membra liquore | hospes Olympiacae seruato more palaestrae*, 4.613–14), while Antaeus pours sand over his body so as to avail himself of his mother's undiluted strength (*ille parum fidens pedibus contingere matrem | auxilium membris calidas infudit harenas*, 4.615–16). In the ensuing contest, the earth is at once the site of the wrestling match (4.626–9) and a participant in the contest (4.629–32, 636–7). She not only restores Antaeus' strength (4.642–3) but even supplies him with her own (*conflixere pares, Telluris uiribus ille | ille suis*, 'they fought as equals, the one with the strength of mother Earth, the other with his own', 4.636–7; cf. 4.651), to such an extent that she too is represented as taking part in the match (*Tellusque uiro luctante laborat*, 'mother Earth struggled as the man fought', 4.644).[54] When Hercules recognises the secret of Antaeus' strength, he moves quickly to sever his opponent's contact with the earth (4.646–7). Held up in the air by Hercules, Antaeus struggles only to return to his mother who can no longer extend her strength to her son (*morientis in artus | non potuit nati Tellus permittere uires*, 4.650–1).

Although Hercules succeeds in enforcing Antaeus' separation from Earth and thereby defeats him, Antaeus and his mother are at least nominally reunited at his death, for the name *Antaei regna* (4.590) marks the site of the contest: *hinc, aeui ueteris custos, famosa uetustas, | miratrixque sui, signauit nomine terras* ('from that contest, antiquity, the guardian of a bygone era who confers renown and admires itself, marked the earth with his name', 4.654–5). Commemoration of the contest under this name records the Libyan monster's challenge to Hercules, alluding to the significance of the name Antaeus, from a Greek word meaning 'opposed, hostile, hateful' (ἀνταῖος) and thence, by extension, 'opponent, enemy'. An implicit etymology deriving the monster's name from ἀντί ('instead of') in combination with αἶα ('earth') may also be heard here, however, for *Antaei regna* marks the site of the contest under the name of the son instead of the mother, and thereby reduces mother Earth from colleague

---

[53] On Lucan's pervasive use of imagery of the arena and gladiatorial combat, see Ahl (1976), 82–115.

[54] *Labor* is characteristically used of the hero's mission: e.g., of Aeneas, Virg. *Aen.* 1.10, 3.393, 6.56; of Hercules, Sil. 3.421; of Paulus at the Battle of Cannae, Sil. 10.232; of the Argonauts, V. Fl. 1.172.

in the contest to inert ground of combat. Indeed, mother Earth herself has vanished from the narrative, for it seems difficult to interpret the poet's final reference to *terras* (at 4.655) as 'mother Earth'.

The elision of mother Earth from the mythical contest here foreshadows the historical subjugation of Libya to Rome. For in a final paradox, Antaeus and the kingdom named for him vanish in the wake of Roman imperial (and cartographic) expansion into Africa. The internal narrator concludes his tale with the observation that the site is better known by the Roman name of *Castra Cornelia*, acquired during the second Punic war:

> sed maiora dedit cognomina collibus istis
> Poenum qui Latiis reuocauit ab arcibus hostem
> Scipio; nam sedes Libyca tellure potito
> haec fuit. en, ueteris cernis uestigia ualli,
> Romana hos primum tenuit uictoria campos.   (4.656–60)

'But the elder Scipio, who summoned the Carthaginian foe back from the Latin citadels, gave a greater name to these very hills; for this was the site at which he camped when he gained Libyan soil. Look, you see traces of the old stockade; Roman victory held these fields first.'

The internal narrator's disdain for the mythical narrative sounds a note of practical Roman contempt for Hercules' failure to capitalise on his own fame in his victory over Antaeus.[55] Through extensive onomastic play the poet underlines the contrast with Roman naming practices on display, for example, in the *Aeneid*, where the Trojan newcomers memorialise their colonisation of Italy cartographically. The *maiora cognomina* ('greater names') which Rome gives to the site punningly allude to Scipio Maior (the 'elder' Scipio, P. Cornelius Scipio Africanus), who not only bestowed his own gentilician name on this part of Africa (i.e., the 'Cornelian Camp', derived from his *nomen*, Cornelius) but himself assumed the cognomen *Africanus* to commemorate his defeat of the Carthaginian army here in 202 BCE.[56] Even in the relentlessly antimythological *Bellum Ciuile*, the feminised ground of epic struggle is subject to the Roman conqueror's overmastering impulse to world domination.

---

[55] Cf. Ahl (1976), 96.
[56] My thanks to Denis Feeney for drawing this complex of puns to my attention.

Like Lucan, who measures the achievements of Caesar against the historical exploits of Hannibal and the mythical labours of Hercules, Silius Italicus sets the deeds of Hannibal in relation to the feats of Hercules throughout the *Punica*. The Herculean standard is especially prominent in the third book of the epic, where Hannibal visits the temple of Hercules at Gades and, gazing on the hero's labours depicted on the temple doors, 'filled his eyes with the varied portrait of his prowess' (*oculos uaria impleuit uirtutis imago*, 3.45). Drawing inspiration from Hercules, Hannibal rehearses the passage of his army over the Alps with a preliminary mountain-climbing manoeuvre in the Pyrenees from which, the poet implies, to survey the extent of his ambition: *at Pyrenaei frondosa cacumina montis | turbata Poenus terrarum pace petebat. | Pyrene celsa nimbosi uerticis arce | diuisos Celtis late prospectat Hiberos* ('but the Carthaginian leader, disturbing the peace of the world, sought the leafy summit of the Pyrenees; from the lofty citadel of her rain-drenched peaks, Pyrene commands a wide prospect and separates the Spanish tribes from the Gauls', 3.415–18; cf. 1.189–92). In crossing the Pyrenees, Hannibal follows closely in Hercules' footsteps, for the Pyrenees take their name from the daughter of the mythical king Bebryx (*nomen Bebrycia duxere a uirgine colles*, 3.420), who entertained Hercules en route to his contest with the monster Geryon.

Silius' account of the origin of the Pyrenees' name emphasises the violence which conjoins imperial gaze with male gaze in the feminisation of landscape. During his brief stay with Bebryx, Hercules rapes his host's daughter Pyrene (3.423–5) and thereby becomes the 'cause of her death' (*letique deus . . . | causa fuit leti miserae deus*, 3.425–6): after she gives birth to a serpent, Pyrene flees her father's house and dies in the desolate mountains, torn apart by wild beasts (3.429–33). Silius suppresses the details of the rape and instead emphasises the violence of the maiden's death, 'as if there were an analogic or developmental relationship between rape and mutilation'.[57] Pyrene's flight to lonely caves (*solis . . . in antris*, 3.429) prefigures the scattering of her mangled limbs in the hills, and initiates the process of her physical assimilation to the mountain range that will bear her name. When Hercules returns, he gathers the maiden's scattered limbs, and laments her untimely death until the cor-

---

[57] Richlin (1992a), 165. On this theme in Ovid's *Metamorphoses*, see Richlin (1992a), 161–5.

dillera, assaulted by his voice (an 'echo' of Pyrene's rape?), re-echoes her name: *at uoce Herculea percussa cacumina montis | intremuere iugis; maesto clamore ciebat | Pyrenen, scopulique omnes ac lustra ferarum | Pyrenen resonant* ('but struck by Hercules' voice, the mountain peaks trembled along their ridges; with mournful cry he shouted "Pyrene", and all the rocks and haunts of the beasts re-echoed "Pyrene"', 3.436–9).[58] The name Pyrene sounds over the peaks until it too is absorbed into the mountains, in an image that tropes the maiden's assimilation to the mountain range. Laying out her limbs in a tomb (*tumulo tum membra reponit | supremum illacrimans*, 3.439–40), Hercules gives Pyrene a memorial (like Caieta's) that inscribes her forever in the landscape of his heroic action: *nec honos intercidet aeuo, | defletumque tenent montes per saecula nomen* ('nor will her fame fall into oblivion over time; the mountains preserve the name of the much-mourned maiden through the centuries', 3.440–1). This exemplum exposes the violence that underwrites the assimilation of the female to the topography of epic.

In his mythological epic of Thebes, Statius exploits the metaphorical significance for Rome which Lucan ascribes to the Theban civil war (*BC* 4.548–51).[59] By returning the setting of Roman epic to Greek myth, Statius can also evoke more easily than Lucan and Silius the association of woman with the primeval topography of earlier Roman epic. Book 4 of the *Thebaid* opens with an Argive army finally assembled to set out for Thebes, but another three books intervene before this force arrives at Thebes and the war gets under way. The immediate cause of the delay is a drought visited upon Nemea by Bacchus in an effort to postpone the assault on his native city of Thebes (4.646–715). Bacchus effects the drought through intermediaries, the Nemean water nymphs, whom he urges to withdraw from the plain of Nemea, promising to restore them to their full watery dignity after they have assisted him (4.693–6). The nymphs are at once overcome with a faint dullness (*ast illis tenuior percurrere uisus | ora situs, uiridisque comis exhorruit umor*, 4.697–8), inaugurating in their own features the transformation of the plain (*protinus Inachios haurit sitis ignea campos: | diffugere undae, squalent fontesque*

---

[58] Philip Hardie notes, *per litteras*, that Hercules' re-echoed cry of 'Pyrene' alludes to the Hylas story, where a *puer delicatus* is absorbed into another feminised landscape.

[59] On Thebes as antitype of, or symbolic stand-in for, Rome in Latin epic at least from the time of Ovid's *Metamorphoses*, see Hardie (1990), 228–30; Henderson (1993), 164–8; and Dominik (1994) 130–80.

lacusque, | et caua feruenti durescunt flumina limo, 'forthwith a blazing thirst exhausts the Argive fields; water flees, springs and pools grow brackish, and hollow river-beds harden with hot mud', 4.699–701). Only the waters of Langia remain unaffected by the drought, in accordance with the god's command (*una tamen tacitas sed iussu numinis undas | haec quoque secreta nutrit Langia sub umbra*, 4.716–17).

Bacchus' stratagem successfully provokes a raging thirst in the Argive troops, and the march to Thebes is halted so that Adrastus can send out scouts to locate water for his soldiers. Instead of water, however, the scouts discover Hypsipyle, wet-nurse to the son of the king of Nemea: *tandem inter siluas – sic Euhius ipse pararat – | errantes subitam pulchro in maerore tuentur | Hypsipylen; illi quamuis et ad ubera Opheltes* ('at last, wandering in the woods – thus Bacchus himself had arranged – they suddenly see Hypsipyle, beautiful in her grief, with Opheltes at her breast', 4.739–41). Verbal echoes of the passage in which Bacchus requests help in devastating the landscape with drought symbolically align Hypsipyle with the water nymphs whose transformation instigates the drought. Hypsipyle's appearance is one of neglect, her hair dishevelled and her clothing inelegant (*neglecta comam nec diues amictu*, 4.743), although an innate dignity can still be faintly discerned in her person (*nec mersus acerbis | extat honos*, 4.744–5). Her demeanour parallels the neglect which overtakes the water nymphs when drought descends on the landscape of Nemea, for their hair too is dishevelled (4.697–8), their dignity, *honos*, also dimmed (4.695). Hypsipyle is modelled generally after the Nemean water nymphs, as the aquatic resonance of *mersus* confirms (4.744). More particularly, the portrait of Langia alone nourishing her waters deep within the forest precisely anticipates that of Hypsipyle alone in the Nemean woods suckling the infant Opheltes. Significantly, the verb used of Langia's care for her waters is *nutrit* (4.717), for which the primary meaning is 'suckle.'

Hypsipyle agrees to lead the army to the spring of Langia, undertaking to enact the metaphorical role of wet-nurse to the Argive troops. However her assistance to the Argives entails abandoning her nursling, the infant Opheltes. Removing him from her own lap, she places him in the lap of the Nemean glade, here assimilated to *tellus*, 'mother Earth' (*at puer in gremio uernae telluris*, 4.786). Statius effects a symbolic parallelism between Hypsipyle and the glade of Nemea with the ascription of the role of nurse to Nemea (4.791–3). With Hypsipyle's help, the Argive forces slake their thirst at the waters of Langia (4.800–13), while Opheltes, by contrast, misses his nurse and her milk (*caram modo lactis egeno | nutricem clangore ciens*, 4.788–9). Book 4 closes with a prayer to the glade of Nemea (*siluarum, Nemea, longe regina uirentum*, 'Nemea, queen far and wide of the verdant woods', 4.825), that echoes Adrastus' invocation of Hypsipyle as goddess of the woodlands (*diua potens nemorum*, 4.746), and further reinforces the symbolic parallelism between Hypsipyle and the landscape of Nemea. When the Argives prepare to leave the spring at the opening of book five, Adrastus thanks Hypsipyle herself as the source of the waters (*tuis . . . undis*, 5.23). The natural resources of the Nemean plain are thus metaphorically embodied in the person of Hypsipyle.

This symbolic interconnection is called into question, however, by the death of Opheltes. Invited by Adrastus to tell her story (5.23–27), Hypsipyle responds with a lengthy account of her Lemnian background (5.28–500), while Opheltes continues to lie, abandoned by his nurse, in another part of the Nemean glade (5.501–4). As he sleeps, a snake born of the Nemean glade (*terrigena serpens*, 5.506) passes the site and kills the infant with a flick of the tail, all unwittingly (5.538–40). Hearing her nursling's cry, Hypsipyle returns to the glade where she discovers the dead infant and Capaneus kills the snake (5.565–78). At the snake's death, Statius describes the mourning of the Nemean plain for the snake it is credited with nurturing: *illum et cognatae stagna indignantia Lernae, | floribus et uernis adsuetae spargere Nymphae, | et Nemees reptatus ager, lucosque per omnes | siluicolae fracta gemuistis harundine Fauni* ('You mourned him angrily, standing pools of kindred Lerna; you mourned him too, Nymphs accustomed to sprinkle him with spring flowers, and you field of Nemea which he crawled over; through all the glades you too mourned him with broken reed, forest-dwelling Fauns', 5.579–82). Statius portrays the serpent, like Opheltes a native of Nemea, at play in the plain of Nemea in much the same way that the infant cavorts when Hypsipyle abandons him (cf. 4.791–3). The poet emphasises the correspondence between the two dead offspring of Nemea by placing Hypsipyle's lament for her nursling after the Nemean glade's lament for the snake and by applying to the infant the imagery he has already rehearsed in connection with the snake (5.588–637). The quasi-maternal fertility of Nemea is symbolically mirrored in Statius' portrait of Hypsipyle in the Nemean glade, but the Lemnian queen ultimately fails to nurture the infant entrusted to her care. This failure to nurture the native offspring of Nemea undoes the generic logic that would require her literal immersion in the plain which she figuratively embodies. Despite their zeal for vengeance (5.660–1), Opheltes' parents are prevented by the Argives from killing Hypsipyle on the spot (5.661–703).

Hypsipyle's anomalous position in Nemea, which differentiates her from Ilia and the other female characters we have considered in this chapter, may furnish an explanation for this striking innovation. She emphasises her Lemnian origins in a lengthy account of her history (5.29–496): the daughter of the Lemnian king Thoas, Hypsipyle alone refrains from slaughtering her male kin in the women's massacre of their menfolk; when her compatriots learn of her father's safety in Chios and her complicity in his departure from Lemnos, she flees to the shore where she is captured by pirates and sold into slavery in Greece. An enslaved exile in Nemea (*exul*, 5.499), Hypsipyle is ultimately denied full identification with her new homeland. In her long narrative, she scarcely refers to her twenty years in Greece (5.465–7). Displaced and never finally integrated into an alien landscape, the Lemnian exile abandons her Nemean nursling and merely guides the Argives, as out of place in Nemea as she is,[60] to Langia.

We may connect the pattern of imagery that alienates both Hypsipyle and the Argives from Nemea (ruled by a king who refuses to take part in the war against Thebes, 5.643–9), with the katabasis of Amphiaraus at the end of book seven and the self-sacrifice of Menœceus at the end of book ten. In both episodes, Statius engages the Greek tradition of the Thebans' autochthonous origin. Myth held that after Cadmus had slain the serpent, a son of Mars, he sowed the serpent's teeth in the earth and thence were born the *Spartoi*, or 'sown men', who immediately fell to the slaughter of one another until the last five struck a truce.[61] Statius attributes a prominent role in Amphiaraus' katabasis to the earth, through whose 'hollow entrails' the Argive seer descends to the underworld (*per caua uiscera terrae | uado diu pendens*, 8.109–10). Throughout the episode, the Theban fields are represented as offering opposition to the invading Argives and support to the indigenous forces. Amphiaraus' comrades

[60] Vessey (1973), 187–9.
[61] Aesch. *Th.*; Eur. *Ph.* 657–8; Ov. *Met.* 3.102–30; Stat. *Theb.* 11.489–90; Apollod. *Bib.* 3.1–2.

shun the site of his katabasis because they distrust the Theban earth (*absistunt turmae, suspectaque tellus | omnibus, infidi miles uestigia campi | circumit, atque auidae tristis locus ille ruinae | cessat et inferni uitatur honore sepulcri*, 8.130–3). Palaemon, in his report of the seer's death to the Argive commander-in-chief, claims that the 'impious ground engulfs our chariots, weapons and warriors' (*currus humus impia sorbet | armaque bellantesque uiros*, 8.141–2) but leaves the Theban troops unharmed since 'the earth recognises her own nurslings' (*tellus agnoscit alumnos, | stat Thebana acies*, 8.149–50). The first act of Thiodamas, who assumes Amphiaraus' duties as seer for the Argive forces, is to appease what the Argives interpret as the anger of *Tellus*, 'mother Earth' (*prima sui documenta, sacerdos | Tellurem placare parat*, 8.296–7). To this end, he invokes in prayer a *Tellus* who fuses the diverse generative powers of the Lucretian *natura creatrix*, *terra*, and *magna mater* (she is *alma*, 8.313) with the transformative powers of the Ovidian *tellus* (8.303–7). Thiodamas' prayer attempts to integrate the alien Argive host into the territory of Thebes through the mediating figure of Amphiaraus, whose immersion in the ground of Thebes effects a lasting impression on Theban topography: in the final book of the poem the site of his descent has become a chasm still visible on the field of battle (*quaerunt . . . an rapti pateat specus auguris*, 12.41–2).

In contrast to the Argives' despair, the Thebans rejoice when the earth engulfs Amphiaraus and rehearse the tale of their autochthonous origin (*hi Cadmum lassamque bouem fetosque cruenti | Martis agros*, 'some tell of Cadmus, the weary heifer, and the fields pregnant with bloody warfare', 8.231–2). Later in the poem, however, the earth requires in turn the death of one of her nurslings. Teiresias reports that the serpent of Mars demands the self-sacrifice of one of the earth-born in exchange for a Theban victory (10.610–15), and Menœceus, a son of Creon, is summoned to his death: *terrigenam cuncto patriae pro sanguine poscunt* ('they demand a son of the earth for all the life of the fatherland', 10.668; cf. 10.762–4). Stabbing himself atop the towers of Thebes, Menœceus purifies the city-walls with his blood before hurling himself into the enemy lines, intent on falling upon the Argive troops (10.774–9). Instead, however, his corpse is lightly borne to the Theban earth in the embrace of Piety and Manly Courage (*ast illum amplexae Pietas Virtusque ferebant | leniter ad terras corpus*, 10.780–1).

In Menœceus' death, as in Amphiaraus' katabasis, Statius exploits the conventional metaphor of a maternal *tellus*, but he ruptures his epic predecessors' naturalisation of the affinity between woman and earth by enveloping male, rather than female, characters in the ground of heroic action. Statius elaborates the gulf between metaphorical and literal motherhood in Eurydice's grief-stricken lamentation for her son Menœceus (*et tandem matri data flere potestas*, 10.792), who goes to his death as the last of the *terrigenae*. Eurydice begins with a strongly-drawn contrast between herself, the mother who reared him, and cruel Thebes, the mother who demanded his death: '*lustralemne feris ego te, puer inclute, Thebis | deuotumque caput uilis ceu mater alebam?*' ('was it, illustrious son, as a sacrificial offering and a life consecrated to savage Thebes that I raised you, like a worthless mother?' 10.793–4). She implicitly characterises Menœceus' suicide as a *deuotio ducis*, the Roman ritual of 'consecration' in battle 'of the general' to the gods of the underworld and mother Earth (*deuotum caput*, 10.794; cf. *saeua piacula bello*, 'cruel atonement for war', 10.799).[62] Charging Menœceus with her own death, in a neat reversal of Thebes' demand for his death (*tu, saeue Menœceu, | tu miseram ante omnes properasti extinguere matrem*, 10.802–3), Eurydice in the end concedes the power and primacy of the metaphor: *quosue ego conceptus aut quae male pignora fudi | tam diuersa mihi? nimirum Martius anguis, | quaeque nouis proauum tellus effloruit armis* ('What offspring did I bring to birth, or what misbegotten child, so different from myself? Of course it is the serpent of Mars and the earth which blossomed with the new arms of our ancestors', 10.805–7). Although Menœceus is the child of her womb, his character proves his autochthonous origin and true line of descent from the snake's teeth sown in *tellus*, mother Earth. Eurydice can recognise no trace of herself, his human mother, in his character (*hinc animi tristes nimiusque in pectore Mauors, | et de matre nihil*, 10.808–9). Lamenting, she is carried by her serving women into her chamber where she sits inattentive to their attempts to console her. Statius leaves her there, maddened by the death of her child, with her gaze fixed on her victorious rival: *non illa diem, non uerba precantum | respicit aut uisus flectit tellure relictos | iam uocis, iam mentis inops* ('she neither looks upon the day nor respects the words of those entreating her, nor bends her fixed gaze from the earth, her voice and reason now lost', 10.818–20).

---

[62] On *deuotio*, see Versnel (1976).

This powerful and disturbing image points up a remarkable tension not usually felt in the familiar metaphor of mother Earth. The Greek myths of autochthony commonly feature a metaphorically maternal landscape, but there is no place for a human mother in that ground. Likewise, agricultural terminology commonly furnishes a metaphorical vocabulary for human sexual relations in Greek literature – indeed, ploughing and sowing are frequent metaphors in the Theban myth, particularly in connection with Jocasta – but the woman is not usually assimilated to the field herself.[63] Lucan's mythological digression in *Bellum Ciuile*, and Ovid's mother Earth in the opening books of the *Metamorphoses*, both adhere to the conventional form of the metaphor. But far more frequently, as in Silius' elaboration of the trope, Latin epic quite literally inscribes women in the mythological ground of heroic action. From Ilia's immersion in the Tiber, through Caieta's burial on the border of Latium and the dream of founding a city on Lavinia, to Pyrene's absorption in the Spanish cordillera and the figural embodiment of the Nemean plain in Hypsipyle, the assimilation of woman to landscape provides fertile ground for Roman epic narrative. Female characters, however, are effectively constrained from taking the field themselves once they are absorbed into the mythological topography of epic.

Roman writers of epic repeatedly feminise the ground of heroic action through the symbolic and literal immersion of specific women in the topography of epic, but the figural immersion of women in the landscape is only a small piece of the epic plot. For once engendered the feminised earth metaphorically gives birth to and fosters the male agents who step to the forefront of these narratives. Thus the figural association of earth with the female body insistently differentiates between women *embodying* the earth and men *emerging* from (Epicurus, Antaeus, the *Spartoi*) and *mastering* (Epicurus, Romulus, Aeneas, Hercules) the primeval landscape. The metaphorical inscription of women in the landscape thereby maps sexual difference as an integral feature of epic order.[64] The pattern of imagery that repeatedly enacts the absorption of female characters into the mythological landscapes of Roman epic appeals to a binary opposition between a feminised nature and a masculinised culture

---

[63] A striking exception at *Odyssey* 5.125–7: 'once beautiful-tressed Demeter, having yielded to her desire, lay in love with Iasion and had intercourse with him in a thrice-turned field.'   [64] Cf. Lotman (1979), discussed by De Lauretis (1984), 116–22.

embedded in the larger social complex of attitudes about gender relations in ancient Rome. Through the inscription of specific women in the primeval landscape, epic dramatises the displacement of woman from the Roman cultural order by fixing her in nature.[65] The absorption of women into the topography of Roman epic thus has wide-ranging implications, playing a supporting role in the work of naturalising historical women's subordination within the Roman social order, authorising male domination of the Roman political order, and legitimating the exclusion of women from the class of subjects who govern the Roman empire.

[65] Cf. De Lauretis (1984) and (1987), and Henderson (1989), 51–4.

4

Exordia pugnae: engendering war

Τί δὲ ἐσφέρωμεν αἱ μήτε ἀρχῆς μήτε τιμῆς μήτε
στρατηγίας μήτε τῆς πολιτείας ὅλως, τῆς ὑμῖν ἐς
τοσοῦτον ἤδη κακοῦ περιμαχήτου, μετέχουσαι;[1]
(Hortensia *ap* App. *BC* 4.33)

> femina siluestres Lapithas, populumque biformem
> turpiter apposito uertit in arma mero.
> femina Troianos iterum noua bella mouere
> impulit in regno, iuste Latine, tuo.
> femina Romanis, etiamnunc Vrbe recenti,
> immisit soceros, armaque saeua dedit.[2]
> (Ov. *Am.* 2.12.19–24)

The destructive potential of war in the twentieth century, encompassing
as it does global annihilation, has endowed critical inquiry into the
Western way of war with a new urgency and stimulated analysis of the
role of war narratives in shaping cultural conceptions of power and
conflict.[3] Critiques of the Western investment in war and war narratives

---

[1] 'Why should we pay taxes when we share in neither power nor honour nor military
command nor citizenship at all, over which you fight already to such disastrous
effect?'

[2] 'A woman disgracefully provoked the wild Lapiths and the biform Centaurs to
weapons when the wine was served. A woman incited the Trojans to wage new wars
a second time in your kingdom, just Latinus. A woman sent fathers-in-law against
Romans, already even in the early city, and provided cruel arms'.

[3] Fundamental are Scarry (1985) and Said (1993). Cf. Huston (1986); Elshtain (1987);
MacDonald, Holden, and Ardener (1987); Henderson (1994), 94–8.

have been increasingly concerned to articulate the complicated nexus of social relations that embed the structure of war within hierarchies of political organisation.[4] The central role Latin epic poetry has played in forming European attitudes to war especially compels classicists to enter a debate often disturbingly ill-informed about 'our' canonical texts, and challenges us to interrogate the complex relations that link war, gender and the engendering of war in battle narratives of the classical epic tradition. Where better to begin to examine the interconnection of gender with warfare, after all, than in the poetry that founds Roman empire and engenders the imperial ambitions of Europe and America?

Current discussion of the interrelation of gender and war in Western literature takes its point of departure from a famous passage in the *Iliad*, where Hector outlines a dichotomy between male and female, combatant and non-combatant, battle-front and home-front, that is often read as a dichotomy between war and peace.[5] 'Go home to your wool-working', Hector bids Andromache after their meeting at the Trojan wall, 'and leave the conduct of war to men' (*Il.* 6.490–3). The violence of war in the *Iliad*, however, cannot be contained within this neat opposition for it continually threatens to spread from the battlefield into the besieged city. Moreover, Hector's formulation is undermined elsewhere in the narrative by recurrent references to the complicity of women with the outbreak of war – in the portrait of Helen as the cause of the Trojan War, in the rehearsals of her role by Chryseis and Briseis, in Andromache's offer of tactical advice to her husband, and in Thetis' gift of arms to her son.[6] It must be stressed, however, that the Homeric ideal of martial glory is expressed in a phrase, κλέα ἀνδρῶν ('famous exploits of men'), that lays bare the androcentrism of the genre. Martial glory is not available to women in Homeric poetry and the poems accordingly have little place for female characters in the war narratives. In the Hellenistic period, Apollonius of Rhodes brilliantly encapsulates the genre's propensity to inscribe woman at the centre of conflict, but leave her out of the narra-

---

[4] Seminal discussion in Scarry (1985), 60–157; see now also Cooper, Munich, Squier (1989).

[5] Arthur (1981); Cooper, Munich, Squier (1989a), 11; *contra* Helms (1989), 26. On the conventional Western association of women with peace and men with war, see Elshtain (1987).

[6] On Helen, see Collins (1988), 41–67; on Andromache, see Arthur (1981); on Thetis, see Cooper, Munich, Squier (1989a), 9–10, and Slatkin (1991).

tive, when he has Jason refuse to allow Atalanta to join the company of the Argonauts 'because he feared terrible conflicts for the sake of love' (*Arg.* 1.773).

The opening words of the *Aeneid* (*arma uirumque cano*, 1.1) invite comparison with the subjects of the *Iliad* and *Odyssey* (the carnage caused by Achilles' wrath and the man of many turns), and simultaneously evoke the central concern of Greek epic song, as *arma uirum* is fleetingly read as a translation of κλέα ἀνδρῶν.[7] Virgil's second prologue (7.37–45) echoes Apollonius' invocation of the Muse Erato midway through the *Argonautica* (3.1–5) and elaborates a traditionally androcentric conception of war in which the clichés of the genre figure prominently (*reges*, 7.37, 42; *pugnae*, 40; *bella*, 41; *acies*, 42; *arma*, 43). The invocation gestures towards a traditional association of marriage with war in Greek epic, and signals in particular Virgil's debt to Apollonius' thematic association of love (ἔρως) with strife (ἔρις) in the *Argonautica*.[8] Nonetheless, the epic clichés of these two proœmia occlude the complex relationship between the gender system and the structure of war which Virgil develops in the *Aeneid*.

A series of *reginae* instigate war in the *Aeneid*. Juno, *regina deum* (1.9, etc.), in her first appearance in the poem savagely contrasts Minerva's success in sinking almost the entire Greek fleet after the Trojan war with her own continuing failure to destroy the Trojans in war: *ast ego, quae diuum incedo regina Iouisque | et soror et coniunx, una cum gente tot annos | bella gero* (1.46–8). The depth of her hatred for the Trojans is emphasised in book 2 when Venus allows Aeneas a glimpse of the divine assault on Troy (2.602–23), and he sees Juno in the forefront of battle, holding the Scaean Gates and summoning the Greek ranks from the ships (*hic Iuno Scaeas saeuissima portas | prima tenet sociumque furens a nauibus agmen | ferro accincta uocat*, 2.612–14). In book 7, when the Trojans have reached Italy and concluded a compact with the Italians, Juno determines if not to prevent settlement (as the fates forbid) at least to provoke a new war and delay the settlement indefinitely (7.317–22). Out of Juno's obsessive efforts to efface Troy down to the last man Virgil generates the narrative action of his poem.

---

[7] Cf. *Aen.* 9.777, where Virgil changes the syntax of the *incipit*, *arma uirum*, from accusative to genitive plural (*uirum* for *uirorum*): see Fowler (1997), 267; and Hardie (1994), 239 and 82 (on *Aen.* 9.57).

[8] *Arg.* 1.773, and 4.445–9. My thanks to Richard Hunter for the second reference.

Helen is also associated with the outbreak of war. Implicitly viewed as the cause of the Trojan War by Aeneas (2.601) and the Sibyl (6.93–4), she is explicitly credited by Deiphobus, her second Trojan husband, with leading the Greek army in its final assault on Troy (*flammam media ipsa tenebat | ingentem et summa Danaos ex arce uocabat*, 6.518–19). Deiphobus even identifies Helen as the author of his death for, he tells Aeneas, she concealed his weapons while he slept (6.523–4) and then invited Menelaus into the house, 'laid open the threshold' to her first husband so that he could kill her third in his bed-chamber (*intra tecta uocat Menelaum et limina pandit*, 6.525). Helen's career of sexual transgression is troped in the socially transgressive action of a militaristic Helen opening one husband's house to another. This woman violates the 'traditional territorial assignments'[9] of both gender and war.

Another warmongering *regina* is Dido, whose deathbed curse calling for unceasing enmity between her people and the descendants of Aeneas affords a myth of origins for the historical Punic wars (4.625–9). Virgil draws on many figures in his portrait of Dido,[10] but within the *Aeneid* itself two models emerge as particularly significant: Penthesilea and Cleopatra. We first see Dido immediately after Aeneas views the Penthesilea-panel in the temple to Juno at Carthage (1.490–7), and this conjunction no less than Venus' prologue (1.340–68) colours our interpretation of her role in the poem. Penthesilea leads a contingent of Amazons against the Greeks at Troy, but her affiliation with the Trojan forces is at most implicit in Virgil's description of her as a warrior-woman who dares to contend with men (*bellatrix, audetque uiris concurrere uirgo*, 1.493). The historical Egyptian queen Cleopatra, another important model for Dido, enters the world of the *Aeneid* in one of the poem's most explicit gestures to the historical relevance of its mythological narrative: she is represented on the shield of Aeneas in the midst of the naval battle at Actium summoning the forces of the East to contend in a conflict of cosmic dimensions (*regina in mediis patrio uocat agmina sistro*, 8.696).[11]

Frequently the *reginae* who instigate conflict in the poem work in association with the Furies as Virgil transforms the avenging Furies (Erinyes,

---

[9] Higonnet (1989), 81, on nineteenth- and twentieth-century European and American civil war novels.
[10] On Dido see Heinze (1993), 95–120 (= (1915), 115–44); Pöschl (1962); Horsfall (1973–4); Monti (1981); Moles (1987); Hunter (1993), 175–82; and Quint (1993), 108–13.   [11] Cf. Hardie (1986), 97–110; Quint (1993), 21–46; Wyke (1992), 106–12.

Eumenides) of Greek literature, along with the punitive *Dirae* ('dread female ones') of Roman religion, into the embodiments of strife in battle and the discord of war (*furor*).[12] Thus the Eumenides sit between War and Discord at the threshold of the underworld (6.279–81); the *Dirae* appear on the shield of Aeneas in the company of Mars, Discord and Bellona at the battle of Actium (8.700–3); and the Fury Tisiphone rages on the battlefield at the very centre of the action in the Italian war (10.760–1). The Furies not only symbolise the violence of war but actively summon 'the man' to battle throughout the poem. Aeneas follows the summons of an Erinys when he rushes into battle during the sack of Troy (2.337–8), and the Trojan and Latin troops muster for war in book 7 at the summons of the Fury Allecto (7.511–22). Dido invokes the *Dirae ultrices*, among other chthonic divinities, to enforce her curse on Aeneas (4.607–10). She herself, however, takes on the attributes of a Fury when she tells Aeneas that she will pursue him even after her death (4.384–7), and again when she calls on an avenger of her race to harry the Trojans by fire and sword, in phrasing that evokes the traditional role of the Greek Furies in avenging crimes (4.625–6).

In the symbolic economy of the *Aeneid*, the very voice of violence and war is female. Thus the Fury Allecto sounds the signal for battle by amplifying her infernal voice on the curved horn of the war trumpet (*de culmine summo | pastorale canit signum cornuqe recuruo | Tartaream intendit uocem, qua protinus omne | contremuit nemus et siluae insonuere profundae*, 7.512–15). Her summons spurs Trojans and Latins to assemble at the sound of her dread horn: *tum uero ad uocem celeres, qua bucina signum | dira dedit, raptis concurrunt undique telis | indomiti agricolae, nec non et Troia pubes | Ascanio auxilium castris effundit apertis* (7.519–22). There is late evidence that the Romans derived *bucina* from *uox*,[13] and Virgil seems to activate this etymology here.

Civil discord in particular is frequently mapped onto the gender system. Nugent has brilliantly analysed the episode in book 5 where the Trojan women fire the Trojan ships (5.605–79), one of many passages in the poem which figuratively dramatise the Roman propensity for civil war, and she has demonstrated Virgil's inscription of conflict between the

---

[12] On the Furies, see Feeney (1991), 163–4, and Hardie (1993), 40–41; on the *Dirae*, see van der Graaf (1945), and Hübner (1970). On *furor* in the *Aeneid*, see Pöschl (1962).

[13] *bucina est qua signum datur in hostem, dicta a uoce, quasi uocina* (Isid. *Orig.* 18.4.1). I thank Philip Hardie for the reference.

sexes at the centre of the episode.[14] The firing of the ships brings to an abrupt end the funeral games for Anchises with the Trojan 'men and boys act[ing] out essential group values', while the Trojan women, segregated from the men, 'are isolated, excluded, and mournful'.[15] The final event in the funeral games is the *lusus Troiae*, 'Trojan game', in which youths trained by Ascanius engage in war-games (5.545–603).[16] When the women fire the ships, the youths' rehearsal for battle is transformed into a real confrontation between Ascanius (5.667–74),[17] backed by Aeneas and the Trojan ranks (*accelerat simul Aeneas, simul agmina Teucrum*, 5.675), and the women (5.676–9) in a challenge to the Trojan leadership that thematically pairs civil conflict with conflict between the sexes.

Similarly, conflict between male and female informs the initial break-down of Italian order in book 7. The narrative displaces the challenge to the established order in Italy posed by the arrival of the Trojans from the external group onto an internal outgroup, reinscribing the potential conflict between Trojans and Latins as a challenge from within Latin society to the traditional territorial assignments of gender. When Latinus' rebellious queen Amata overturns his house (*omnemque domum uertisse Latini*, 7.407) by fleeing to the woods in a Bacchic frenzy (7.385–91, 404–5) she initiates the breakdown of order in his city. Rumours of Amata's activity in the forest inspire the Latin matrons to desert their homes in the city and follow her into the woods (*fama uolat furiisque accensas pectore matres | idem omnis simul ardor agit noua quaerere tecta. | deseruere domos*, 7.392–4). The figural evocation of civil discord in Latinus' city is confirmed by situational echoes of the Trojan women's flight into the woods after the firing of the ships (5.677–8). In both episodes the women's actions are aligned with insurrection.

Virgil's thorough-going inscription of gender in the structure of war is illustrated in the two conflicts that frame the proto-Roman experience and understanding of war in the *Aeneid*, the battle with the Harpies (the first battle narrative after the sack of Troy, 3.209–67), and the outbreak of the Italian war in book 7. The encounter with the Harpies, well known

---

[14] Nugent (1992).   [15] Nugent (1992), 267.

[16] Augustus revived these equestrian manoeuvres for noble youth (which Julius Caesar had also celebrated, Suet. *Jul.* 39.2), putting on frequent performances as part of his renovation of Roman morality and 're-establishment' of 'traditional' values (*Aug.* 43.2).   [17] On Ascanius' generalship in this scene, see Nisbet (1990), 55–6.

to be a Virgilian innovation in the Aeneas-legend, furnishes an exemplary test-case for analysis of the interpenetration of the gender system with the structure of war. The Furies' central role in the poem's war narratives is sharply focused in the episode, for the Harpies are assimilated to the Furies and the *Dirae* throughout.[18] Aeneas characterises the Harpies as monstrous figures at home in Hell (*tristius haud illis monstrum, nec saeuior ulla | pestis et ira deum Stygiis sese extulit undis*, 3.214–15), where Virgil explicitly locates them later in the poem in a company that includes the Furies (6.289). In book 3 the Harpies' leader even claims for herself the title 'greatest of the Furies' (*Furiarum . . . maxima*, 3.252). The keynote of the episode is sounded in the repetition of the adjective *dirus*, 'dread' (3.211, 228, 235, 256, 262; cf. 713), which forges a link between the Harpies and the *Dirae*. Aeneas' description of the Harpies as *pestis et ira deum* ('plague and anger of the gods', 3.215) is a characteristically Virgilian allusion to etymological speculation deriving *Dira* from *dei ira*.[19]

Among Virgil's most striking innovations in the episode is his insistence on the Harpies' bellicosity.[20] Twice the Trojans institute a feast and invite Jupiter (3.222–4, 229–31), and twice the Harpies attack suddenly and unexpectedly to despoil the meal (3.225–8, 232–4). Their violent character is underscored by the description of their clashing wings (*magnis clangoribus*, 3.226; *sonans*, 3.233) and noisy approach (*ergo ubi delapsae sonitum per curua dedere | litora*, 3.238–9) in vocabulary that evokes the din of battle at Troy (2.313, 338). In response to their attacks, Aeneas declares war (*dira bellum cum gente gerendum*, 3.235) and marshals his troops (*dat signum specula Misenus ab alta | aere cauo. inuadunt socii et noua proelia temptant*, 3.239–40; cf. 3.234–7). Within Roman cultural conventions, the militant female necessarily constitutes a disruptive force. An infernal brood of bird-women in whom contagion and pollution are embodied, the Harpies physically emblematise the socially transgressive character of the militaristic female: *uirginei uolucrum uultus, foedissima uentris | proluuies uncaeque manus et pallida semper | ora fame* ('maiden's faces on birds, foulest slime oozing from their bellies, hooked

---

[18] Cf. Rabel (1985), 319–20.

[19] See Maltby (1991) s.v. *dirus*, and cf. O'Hara (1996), 240 on *Aen.* 12.845–52.

[20] Contrast the characterisation of the Harpies as winds and hounds in Ap. Rhod. 2.267–86, on which see Hunter (1993), 81, 130–1.

hands, and faces always pale with hunger', 3.216–18). The first challenge to the Trojan mission neatly embeds gender in the structure of war.[21]

A similar pattern, vastly magnified, emerges in the scenes that stage the outbreak of the Italian war in book 7.[22] A prominent trend in recent Virgilian criticism has emphasised the poet's 'studied refusal to assign individual human responsibility for the outbreak of hostilities'[23] in the Italian war. Such criticism, however, fails to account for the work of gender in the Virgilian discourse of war. We may focus our interrogation on the scene where Allecto arrives at the palace of Turnus to stir up trouble in Ardea (7.406–14). Disguised as Calybe, an aged priestess of Juno, Allecto urges the sleeping Turnus to take up arms and defend the priority of his marriage alliance with Latinus (7.429–34). Turnus counters the alarmist counsel of a figure whom he takes to be an old woman with the patronising advice that she confine herself to her religious duties and leave the conduct of war to men, since wars are waged by men: *bella uiri pacemque gerent quis bella gerenda* (7.444). These words echo Hector's parting admonition to Andromache to leave war to men (*Il.* 6.492–3) and situate Turnus within the traditional ideology of Greek epic that defines masculine martial glory as the subject of the genre. But in a radical departure from Greek epic decorum, Allecto utterly overturns the Homeric distinction Turnus would maintain: *respice ad haec: adsum dirarum ab sede sororum,* | *bella manu letumque gero* ('look at this: I am come from the seat of the dread sisters, and I carry wars and death in my hand', 7.454–5). Critics generally interpret Allecto's role here as an external manifestation of Turnus' internal psychological state, revealing to Turnus (and to the reader) Turnus' own latent desire for war, and her response to Turnus has accordingly been read as 'an intensification' of the views expressed by him.[24] Far from intensifying Turnus' meaning,

---

[21] The collective Trojan conflict with the Harpies contrasts strikingly with the heroic individualism of the Boreads' encounter with them in Apollonius of Rhodes (2.263–90). On the corporate nature of the proto-Roman mission, see Vance (1973), Nugent (1992), and Quint (1993), 23–31 and 90–6.

[22] See Fredricksmeyer (1985), 233 n.15, and Vance (1973); cf. Heinze (1993), 148–55 (= (1915), 182–93).

[23] Horsfall (1987), 49. Cf. Feeney (1991), 171–2; Pöschl (1962), 92–5.

[24] Fraenkel (1990), 261; cf. Williams (1983), and Fredricksmeyer (1985), 232, with further bibliography, n.12. *Contra* Heinze (1993), 152–3 (= (1915), 187–9; Pöschl (1962), 91–3; Feeney (1991), 168–71.

however, Allecto's words here effectively contradict him, for she opposes *sorores* (7.454) to his *uiri* (7.444) and replaces his *pacem* (7.444) with her own *bella* (7.455). Her words reveal her to be the literal 'disturber of the peace' in Italy, in a formulation that explicitly aligns woman with death and warfare, and leaves to man by implication life and peace. This crucial exchange renders visible the poem's displacement of the violent summons of war from male to female characters.

The opposing views of Turnus and Allecto illuminate the role of gender in the structure of the poem's war narratives, and the scenes that dramatise the outbreak of war in book 7 sweepingly confirm Allecto's summation. The noun *bellum*, 'war', occurs for the first time after the invocation to Erato in a passage that locates the origins of the war in the person of the Italian princess Lavinia. As her father Latinus performs ritual sacrifice at the altar, Lavinia's hair bursts into flames that glow throughout the palace (7.71–7). Many readers have remarked the parallels between this scene in book 7 and a scene in book 2 in which Ascanius is the recipient of a similar prodigy (2.680–91). Similar as the passages are, however, the differences between the scenes are equally instructive: 'Lavinia's flame is less optimistic in its symbolism. Instead of light, [hers] gives off a dark smoke; it is violent rather than holy; and far from licking her [temples] gently, it seems to "consume" the princess and to spread uncontrollably throughout the palace. Clearly, Virgil means to emphasize the destructive aspect of the portent.'[25] Verbal details of the description of the prodigy connect Lavinia's flame with the fires that consume Troy and Carthage, for she scatters flames through her father's halls (7.76–7) in an image which prefigures the fall of his citadel (12.672–5) and symbolically aligns Lavinia not only with Helen as she is portrayed by Deiphobus, brandishing a torch and summoning the Greek army to the sack of Troy (6.518–19), but also with Dido, whose funeral pyre lights up the whole city of Carthage (5.3–5; cf. 4.669–71). To be sure, 'Lavinia is the passive *locus* for this fire imagery, Helen its active initiator, Dido on her pyre both passive victim and active originator, through her curse, of the flames of war prefigured by the pyre.'[26] Virgil explains the prodigy as portending for Lavinia an illustrious future but for her countrymen war (*namque fore inlustrem fama fatisque canebant | ipsam, sed*

---

[25] Reckford (1961), 259.   [26] Philip Hardie (*per litteras*).

populo magnum portendere bellum, 7.79–80), and a causal connection is generally felt in the passage. This is confirmed by the rhetorical impetus of the second half of the *Aeneid* which represents the *result* of the war in Italy, a dynastic marriage, as its *cause*, the first of the *exordia pugnae.*

The first skirmish multiply overdetermines woman's primacy in the engendering of war. Spying Ascanius out on the hunt, Allecto maddens his (female) hounds (*rabidae canes*, 7.493–4) in pursuit of a magnificent (male) stag (*ceruus*, 7.483) which has been partially domesticated by Latinus' chief herdsman and his sons (7.476–95). But the stag is especially dear to their sister Silvia, and so it is she who summons the Italians to help: *Siluia prima soror palmis percussa lacertos | auxilium uocat et duros conclamat agrestis* ('their sister Silvia beating her breast with her palms, was the first to summon aid and call together the hardy peasants', 7.503–4). The Fury's final contribution to Juno's war effort thus exemplifies the inscription of gender in the structure of war: the Italian war's pretext is trebly female-authored (Allecto, the hounds, Silvia), its dupes trebly male (Ascanius, the stag, the Italian troops, 7.504–10).[27]

The distinction between ruthless female instigation and helpless male prosecution of war is carefully maintained in the formal outbreak of the Italian war: Allecto sounds the trumpet that summons the troops to war (7.511–22) while the queen of the gods arrogates to herself the formal initiation of hostilities when she flings wide the Gates of War: *tum regina deum caelo delapsa morantis | impulit ipsa manu portas, et cardine uerso | Belli ferratos rumpit Saturnia postis* (7.620–2; cf. 7.572–3, 592). So also in book 12, a second compact between Trojans and Latins is ruptured and a second conflict engendered, through the violent militarism of Juno and Juturna. As the two sides prepare a truce and agree to abide by the results of the single combat between Turnus and Aeneas, Juno sends Juturna onto the battlefield to reopen hostilities (12.134–60). Juturna infiltrates the Italian ranks in the guise of Camertus, sowing dissension and renewing desire for battle among the Italians (12.222–310). Like Allecto in book 7, it is Juturna in book 12 who gives the signal that sends the Italian troops rushing into war (12.244–69; cf. 7.511–22). If then Virgil does indeed plot a studied refusal to assign individual human responsibility for the outbreak of the Italian war, he does so very specifically by displac-

[27] Cf. Fredricksmeyer (1985), 233 n.15.

ing responsibility for a conflict between massed armies of men onto the militaristic regimen of the female.[28]

In a neat symmetry, the representational strategy that aligns woman with war aligns 'the man' with peace. Although there are hints that war is not unknown to Italy (7.423–6, 8.55), Latinus is explicitly introduced as a king whose rule has overseen a lengthy peace (*rex arua Latinus et urbes | iam senior longa placidas in pace regebat*, 7.45–6; cf. 11.252–4). Unlike Dido, who is manipulated by both Mercury and Venus to ensure her hospitable reception of Aeneas in Carthage (1.297–304, 657–94), he welcomes the Trojans on his own initiative (7.192–204). Aeneas instructs the Trojan embassy to sue for peace (*pacemque exposcere*, 7.155), and although Ilioneus' actual petition is for a small plot of land on the shore (7.229–30), Latinus responds with offers of political alliance and peaceful settlement (7.263–6) and concludes the negotiations by pledging his daughter to the Trojan leader in a dynastic marriage (7.267–73), and bestowing gifts on the Trojans (7.274–83). Notwithstanding the ironies inherent in the gift of war-horses, the Trojan embassy is represented as returning to the camp with peace: *talibus Aeneadae donis dictisque Latini | sublimes in equis redeunt pacemque reportant* (7.284–5). This accords with the intentions of both Aeneas (7.155) and Latinus (7.266) as they are specified in the narrative.[29] Consistent with this portrayal of Latinus as a king devoted to the ideal of peace is his refusal to be swayed from marrying Lavinia to Aeneas by Amata (7.357–74), and his lengthy warning to Turnus against prosecuting the war (7.585–600). Latinus is last glimpsed resisting Italian pressure to throw open the *Belli Portae* in an official declaration of war (7.616–19).

Although the Italians pursue a policy of peace by no means as energetically as Aeneas does in the second half of the poem, Latinus is not the only Italian leader to try to resist the summons of the female advocates

---

[28] The Trojan forces in Italy are all male, although at least one woman, Euryalus' mother, remains in the Trojan band even after the purge of the weak in *Aeneid* 5; by contrast, the Italian forces are supported on occasion by their womenfolk (11.891–5), and feature the Italian huntress Camilla (7.803–17, 11.498–868) at the head of a contingent of Amazon-like warrior-women (11.655–63).

[29] For Aeneas' commitment to peaceful settlement, cf. 11.108–19, 12.107–12, 175–94, and see Lyne (1983a); for Latinus', cf. 7.598–9, 11.230–8, 300–35, 469–72, 12.19–45, 195–211.

of war. As we have seen, Turnus declines to follow the disguised Allecto's advice and enter into armed conflict with the Trojans (7.425–44), at least until he is set upon by the Fury and fired for war by her torch (7.456–66). Although he then becomes the most vocal proponent of war,[30] after Juno and her tools, that does not prevent other Italian leaders from contesting the war. Galaesus, for example, is singled out as a peace-maker on the Italian side (7.535–6), even though he dies in the first skirmish of the war (7.535–9), and in book 11 Drances emerges as a vocal, if discreditable, advocate for peaceful settlement (11.336–75). Furthermore, there is an implicit connection between Latinus and Aeneas, on the one hand, in their energetic pursuit of peace and particularly in Latinus' refusal to open the Gates of War, and the *princeps* Augustus, on the other hand, whose close association with peace and the closing of the Gates of War is proclaimed at the outset of the poem in Jupiter's promise to Venus (1.286–96).[31] Jupiter's prophecy opposes the madness of war, *furor* (the essence of the Furies), to 'everything that makes for peace, civilized Empire, and justice'.[32] The narrative links Jupiter, on the divine level, Aeneas on the mythological, and Caesar's adoptive son Augustus, on the historical, as the legitimate authors of and authorities on *pax* and order. On the shield of Aeneas, Augustus stands on the lofty ship-deck (*stans celsa in puppi*, 8.680) – a posture assumed by both Anchises and Aeneas elsewhere in the poem (3.527, 4.554, 10.261, 12.564) – in defence of the Roman order of peace and patriarchy (8.678–81, 714–28) against the representatives of Eastern disorder and female rule, Antony and Cleopatra (685–713).[33] The shade of Anchises authorises not only Aeneas' imperial project but also his descendants' everlasting empire with the justification of Roman peace: *tu regere imperio populos, Romane, memento | (hae tibi erunt artes), pacique imponere morem, | parcere subiectis et debellare superbos* ('Roman [man], remember to rule peoples in empire, (these will be your skills), to impose custom on peace, to spare the conquered and battle down the proud', 6.851–3). His words fall squarely within the traditional parameters of Roman discussion of imperialism: since the end, a Roman settlement (*pax*), justifies the means, war (*bellum*) can be redescribed as peace, as in *paco*, 'impose a settlement on', or *pacifico*, 'make

---

[30] Cf. 7.467–75, 577–9, 596–7, 11.376–444, 459–67, 12.1–4, *passim*.

[31] Cf. Aug. *Anc.* 13. Powell (1992a), 163, analyses links between Latinus and Augustus.

[32] Lyne (1983a), 320.   [33] Quint (1993), 21–49.

peace on'.[34] Thus the men who wage war in the *Aeneid* emerge as the proponents of peace, while the advocacy of war is displaced onto a series of militant women.

The conclusion should not be startling but scholars have often denied it,[35] or more commonly they have simply ignored the structural importance of gender to the war narratives of the *Aeneid*. They may have been encouraged to do so because in the end the poem cannot sustain an unproblematic inscription of conflict between the sexes at the heart of the structure of war. Towards the end of book 12, Juno abandons her opposition to the integration of the Trojans and Italians, and quits the fray (12.841–2). Conflict continues, however, in the duel between Aeneas and Turnus; and in a profoundly unsettling reprise of Juno's characteristic role in the poem, it is Jupiter who sends down to the arena of combat one of the twin *Dirae*, who bring death and destruction to men and cities at his bidding (12.849–52).[36] Finally, when Aeneas slaughters Turnus (12.945–52), bringing the poem to a close and inaugurating centuries of Roman warfare, he is inflamed by the very anger and battle-lust (*furiis accensus et ira | terribilis*, 12.946–7) that animate Juno (*saeuae memorem Iunonis ob iram*, 1.4) and the Furies throughout the poem.[37] It proves far easier to initiate conflict in the *Aeneid* than to bring it to an end.

The baldric of Pallas, the sight of which inspires Aeneas to kill Turnus at the end of the poem (12.941–4), furnishes a final emblem of the interrelation of gender and war in the *Aeneid*. As Turnus strips it from Pallas' corpse, Virgil describes the scene engraved thereon: *impressumque nefas: una sub nocte iugali | caesa manus iuuenum foede thalamique cruenti* ('a tale of infamy embossed upon it: on one wedding night, a band of youths foully cut down, the marriage-chambers bloodied', 10.497–8). In interpreting the symbolism of Pallas' baldric by comparison with its Homeric model, the baldric of Heracles on which are emblazoned wild animals

---

[34] On the relationship of *Aen.* 6.851–3 to Roman justification of imperialism, see Lyne (1983a); on Roman imperialism, see Brunt (1978), Finley (1978), Harris (1979), Rich and Shipley (1993). On *paco*, *pax*, and *pacifico*, see Harris (1979), 35–6 and Woolf (1993), and cf. Aug. *Anc.* 25–6; on the 'just war', see Harris (1979), 166–75. On 'redescription' as a constitutive feature of the grammar of war, see Scarry (1985), 72–8.

[35] Vance (1973), 121; Fredricksmeyer (1985), 233 n.15; Wiltshire (1989), 38–55 and 107–21.

[36] Cf. Hardie (1993), 73, noting that '*Dei ira*, the just anger of Jupiter, turns out to be a *Dira*, a Fury'.   [37] Putnam (1994), 187.

and murderous battles (*Od.* 11.609–12), critics have sought to establish 'some reference to both Turnus as slayer and Pallas as slain'.[38] Accordingly, they have attended to the Argive setting of the myth with its implicit reference to Turnus' Argive descent, and to the theme of *mors immatura* with its symbolic resonance in the early deaths of both Pallas and Turnus.[39] Undiscussed is the thematisation of conflict between the sexes on the baldric. Yet the killing of the sons of Aegyptus by their cousins the Danaids, on their wedding night, neatly emblematises the pervasive inscription of conflict between the sexes in the structure of war in the *Aeneid*, right down to its specification of marriage as the occasion which enmeshes the man in conflict.

The relentless displacement of responsibility for murderous conflict between men onto the transgressive figure of the militant woman in the *Aeneid* shows several points of contact with the propaganda of Octavian against Antony in the years before and immediately after the battle of Actium in 31 BCE.[40] In this period, Octavian's propaganda redescribes civil war between Roman strongmen as a conflict between a feminised East, represented by the Egyptian queen who has enslaved Antony and threatens to enslave all Roman men, and a masculine West, represented by Octavian, the 'son' of Caesar who restores liberty to Rome by conquering Cleopatra.[41] Certainly, the figure of the Egyptian queen informs Virgil's portrait of Dido in the first half of the *Aeneid*, as well, of course, as his representation of the queen in the battle of Actium on the shield of Aeneas. But Cleopatra alone can hardly explain the urgency with which the figure of the militaristic female recurs in the war narratives of the *Aeneid*, particularly in the scenes of civil conflict among Trojans and Italians (and between them). Rather, the Virgilian pattern of imagery should be related to the contemporary circulation of discourses concerning the unprecedented visibility of upper class Roman women in the political upheavals of the decade after Caesar's assassination.[42]

---

[38] Harrison (1991), 198.

[39] See Conte (1986), 185–93; Fowler (1987); and Putnam (1994), on the symbolism of the baldric.

[40] See Hallett (1977), Henderson (1987), Wyke (1992), 112–21, and Quint (1993) 29 on the description of Actium in *Aeneid* 8; and cf. Joshel (1992) on Livy.

[41] Hamer (1993), 20–3; cf. Wyke (1992), and Henderson (1987), 113.

[42] Roman authors consistently associate the visibility of women in the political realm with the breakdown of order in the Roman state: see Edwards (1993), 34–62; Hillard (1989); Joshel (1997); and Wyke (1989).

The historian Appian reports that in 42 BCE the Triumvirs proposed to raise money for the coming conflict with the Republican forces of Brutus and Cassius by levying a tax on the property of 1400 Roman *matronae* (*BC* 4.32–4), wealthy relations of the proscribed. In response to this threat, the *matronae* made delegations *en masse* to the womenfolk of the Triumvirs. Such a course of action, with the women working to effect change through the female relations of important men, was socially sanctioned at Rome. But according to Octavian's propaganda, which Appian follows, a breakdown in social propriety occurred: although the *matronae* were hospitably received by Octavian's sister and Antony's mother, they were so rudely treated by Antony's wife Fulvia that they staged a demonstration in the Forum to confront the Triumvirs directly. The *matronae* thus resorted to public and direct action when Antony's woman failed to adhere to the code of conduct becoming the wife of a Roman magnate. Before the Triumvirs' tribunal Hortensia delivered an impassioned speech against the proposed tax. The content of Hortensia's speech, no longer extant, is preserved in Greek in Appian's history (part of which is quoted in the first epigraph to this chapter), and conforms to Roman cultural standards of female propriety. But the very fact that Hortensia delivered a speech on a political subject at all in the Forum, the site *par excellence* of Roman political activity, is represented as constituting a profound challenge to Roman norms of female propriety. In the following decade, Octavian's propaganda records numerous such challenges to Roman protocols of female behaviour.

Octavian's defeat of Antony at Actium has ensured Fulvia's reputation as the most infamous example of a Roman woman active in the public (i.e., male) sphere in this period. A central stratagem of the Augustan restoration after Actium was to direct blame for the triumviral proscriptions of 43 and their aftermath on to Lepidus and Antony while depicting Octavian and members of his family as the saviours of as many citizens as possible.[43] It is in the context of Augustan apologetic, therefore, that we should interpret the assignment to Fulvia of responsibility for precipitating the demonstration of the *matronae* in the Forum. In the crisis of the Perusine War of 41, Fulvia was also one of the targets of Octavian's propaganda.[44] Martial preserves an epigram composed by Octavian during the war, in which he taunts Fulvia with Antony's recent infidelity and concludes that Fulvia has gone to war as a substitute for sex (Mart.

[43] Delia (1991), 201.   [44] Hallett (1977); Delia (1991), 203–6.

11.20). Similarly, sling bullets of the Caesarian forces used in the war were inscribed with obscenities suggesting sexual assault on Fulvia. The bullets, like the epigram, redescribe a war fought between massed armies of Roman men under the command of Roman strongmen as a battle between the sexes, with Fulvia cast in the role of sexually insatiable woman to Octavian's self-representation as the virile man who masters her and thereby restores the 'natural' hierarchy of gender at Rome.[45]

Hortensia and Fulvia, who both belonged to the old Republican Roman aristocracy which found itself ranged in opposition to Octavian's forces after the assassination of Caesar, by no means exhaust the examples of Roman women who are represented as participants in the political machinations of the period. Valerius Maximus celebrates two upper class Roman women who succeeded in protecting both their husbands and their husbands' property from Triumviral depredation (Val. Max. 6.7.2–3), while a contemporary funerary eulogy of a Roman matron by her husband commemorates her single-minded devotion to his welfare during the proscriptions (*ILS* 8393). The widower credits his wife with devising him a secure hiding place, providing him in his exile with money and slaves despite being herself under surveillance, and petitioning two of the Triumvirs for her husband's return and full reinstatement.

Livia herself, later Octavian's wife, is reported to have negotiated with Octavian for the safe passage of her first husband, Tiberius Claudius Nero, and their child in flight from Italy after the Perusine War. In the course of the following decade Octavian's sister Octavia and wife Livia come into increasing prominence. The marriage of Octavia to Antony late in 40, for example, is alluded to in Virgil's Fourth Eclogue and commemorated on coins with the partners' portraits minted in the East in 39 and 38. In the following decade Octavian's propaganda promoted a portrait of Octavia as a mediator between the two uneasy allies and a paragon of domestic virtue.[46] In 35 BCE, both Octavia and Livia received grants of tribunician sacrosanctity and freedom from *tutela*, political and financial rights reserved exclusively for men in ancient Rome. The political significance of the grants was further underscored by the public dedication of statues to the two women, an unprecedented award.[47] These novel honours distinguish the womenfolk of the *princeps* for their exemplary compliance with specifically feminine modes of behaviour.

---

[45] Delia (1991), 216 n. 74, citing Hallett (1977), 154–63.

[46] Delia (1991), 206–7 and 216–17 n. 77.   [47] Flory (1993).

The prominence of upper class Roman women in the politics of the decade between Philippi and Actium, and Octavian's propaganda about such women, offer several points of contact with Virgil's representation of social disorder and its causes in the *Aeneid*. The male conquest of the militant female in the *Aeneid* reflects a potent enabling fiction of the early Augustan regime, in which Roman Order is re-established externally through the defeat of Cleopatra and internally through the re-domestication of Roman women. As Jane Marcus argues in connection with the propaganda issuing from the British War Office in the Great War, 'the repression of the male authority figures and displacement of their roles as killers onto the militant and militaristic [female] figure is a precise reading of the cultural needs of the warmongers'.[48] The urgency with which the hierarchy of gender informs the structure of war in the *Aeneid* reflects the social and political uncertainties of the period in which it was written, uncertainties which are in some measure diffused over the course of Augustus' unpredictably long, stable and stabilising rule. As the Actian moment receded, however, the filiation of women with conflict in the poem's war narratives was familiarised and naturalised through the elevation of the *Aeneid* to a central place in the Roman literary and educational establishments.[49] At the same time, the institutionalisation of the Principate resulted in a shift of power from senators to *princeps*, Senate to *Domus Augusta*,[50] with the concomitant rise in the visibility of women in the imperial household commemorated in the historical and biographical narratives of Tacitus and Suetonius. Thus the complex network of gender relations that articulates the structure of war in the *Aeneid*, and the unresolved tensions that they set in play, invite continual renegotiation in later Latin epic.

In the *Metamorphoses* Ovid returns repeatedly to the Virgilian economy of war he had elegantly adapted for elegy in the lines which furnish the second epigraph to this chapter, although in accordance with the thematic programme of a poem whose central preoccupation is flux he disdains systematic development of the trope. In his 'Iliad', Ovid undertakes an extensive and sympathetic analysis of Virgil's contamination of the hierarchy of gender with the structure of war. At the opening of book 12, Paris inaugurates hostilities by bringing war along with a

---

[48] Marcus (1989), 146.
[49] See chapter 2 for the place of the *Aeneid* in the curriculum.
[50] Corbier (1995), Joshel (1997).

stolen wife to the Troad (*qui rapta longum cum coniuge bellum | attulit in patriam*, 12.5–6), in a formulation that is faithful to Virgilian precedent in assimilating woman to war. Ovid downplays the thematic significance of the battle of the sexes in the structure of the Trojan war, however, by focusing his narrative on the male participants and omitting any mention of female *agents provocateurs* or warriors. Indeed he does not connect the return of Helen with the conclusion of the war in book 12, and he omits her altogether from his account of the destruction of Troy in book 13. Only once does he link her return to the goals of the war, when Ulysses includes in his speech about his right to Achilles' arms a brief reference to his embassy to Troy to demand Helen and booty as the price of war (*praedamque Helenamque reposco*, 13.200). Yet the Virgilian paradigm is not so much dismantled as it is submerged in the ensuing narrative.

During a respite from the fighting, the Greek chieftains celebrate a feast one evening at which conversation turns to the subject of virility (*uirtus . . . loquendi | materia est*, 12.159–60), and their own martial exploits, the very stuff of epic (*pugnas referunt hostisque suasque, | inque uices adita atque exhausta pericula saepe | commemorare iuuat*, 12.160–2). Of particular interest to the Greek heroes is the recent death of Cycnus at Achilles' hands, and especially the astonishing fact that Cycnus' body could not be opened up to death by the gash of spear or sword (*uisum mirabile cunctis, | quod iuueni corpus nullo penetrabile telo | inuictumque a uulnere erat ferrumque terebat*, 12.165–7). The only similarly invincible hero any of the assembled warriors can recall is Nestor's old friend from the Calydonian boar hunt (8.305), Caeneus – who was born a woman.

> . . . sic Nestor ait: 'uestro fuit unicus aeuo
> contemptor ferri nulloque forabilis ictu
> Cycnus. at ipse olim patientem uulnera mille
> corpore non laeso Perrhaebum Caenea uidi,
> Caenea Perrhaebum, qui factis inclitus Othryn
> incoluit, quoque id mirum magis esset in illo,
> femina natus erat.'   (*Met.* 12.169–75)

Nestor spoke thus: 'In your generation Cycnus was unique in scorning the sword, unpierceable by a blow. But I myself once saw the Thessalian Caeneus suffer a thousand wounds though he remained physically unharmed; Caeneus of Thessaly, who dwelt on

Mount Othrys and was renowned for his exploits, a fact that was all the more amazing in him, because he had been born a woman.'

Implicit in the military vocabulary Nestor employs is a 'natural' hierarchy of gender that constructs the female body as vulnerable to penetration by the male: if Cycnus' exemplary heroic (male) body was open to no weapon (12.166, 170), how could Caeneus, born with a woman's violable body, remain unhurt after suffering a thousand wounds?[51]

This gendered stereotype informs Nestor's narrative throughout. The beautiful Caenis is the object of numerous suitors' determined but unsuccessful courtship (12.189–96), until Neptune rapes her. Nestor moves from the warrior Caeneus who suffers a thousand wounds (*patientem uulnera mille*, 12.171), to the maiden Caenis who suffers Neptune's violence (*aequorei uim passa dei est*, 12.197) and requests a sex change so as never to suffer such an outrage again ('*magnum' Caenis ait 'facit haec iniuria uotum, | tale pati iam posse nihil; da, femina ne sim*', 12.201–2). Caeneus' masculine invulnerability is contrasted with, and yet constructed upon, Caenis' feminine vulnerability to violence. Nestor, and Caenis, use the verb *pati* to describe the rape (12.197, 202), as Nestor uses it to describe Caeneus' battle endurance (12.171).[52] In addition to the sex change, Neptune bestows imperviousness to the sword on Caeneus, a final gift that fits him out for such manly pursuits (*studiisque uirilibus*, 12.208) as the battle of Centaurs and Lapiths.

In the *Metamorphoses* this battle functions as a narrative doublet of the Trojan war (12.64–145, 580–628), which it displaces from the centre to the margins of book 12 and overshadows in length (12.210–537). Like the Trojan war, the battle of Lapiths and Centaurs begins with bride-theft when the centaur Eurytus snatches Hippodamia from her new husband Pirithous at the wedding feast (12.219–23) and the other centaurs ravish her bridal attendants (12.224–6). The Centaurs' rampage thematically parallels Paris' rape of Helen, just as the Centaurs' abuse of the generous hospitality of their hosts, Pirithous and the Lapiths, echoes Paris' disregard for the courtesy owed to his hospitable host, Menelaus.[53] Both conflicts also feature a seemingly invulnerable hero ultimately defeated in combat and transformed into a bird (Cycnus, 12.70–146; Caeneus,

---

[51] On penetration in Latin sexual terminology, see Adams (1982) 149–51.
[52] On the terminology, see Adams (1982) 189–90, 198–9, and 223.
[53] On this theme in Greek myths concerning the Centaurs, see DuBois (1982), 28–9.

12.459–535), and are further connected by narrative setting, for it is during the truce that follows Achilles' killing of Cycnus that Nestor narrates the battle of Centaurs and Lapiths.

Caeneus comes to prominence in the battle with the Centaurs towards the end of Nestor's catalogue of Lapith heroes, after he has already slain five of the horse-men (12.459–60). This record does not prevent his sixth opponent, the Centaur Latreus, from taunting him with a woman's weakness: *et te, Caeni, feram? nam tu mihi femina semper, | tu mihi Caenis eris. nec te natalis origo | commonuit, mentemque subit, quo praemia facto | quaque uiri falsam speciem mercede pararis?* ('Do I have to put up with you too, Caenis? For you will always be a woman to me, you will always be Caenis to me. Does your natal origin not remind you, does it not enter your mind, for what deed, at what price, you obtained as your reward the deceptive mien of a man?', 12.470–3). Moreover he imitates Turnus (*Aen.* 7.444, echoing Hector, *Il.* 6.492–3) to advise Caeneus to leave the fighting to men: *quid sis nata, uide, uel quid sis passa, columque, | i, cape cum calathis et stamina pollice torque; | bella relinque uiris* ('Look at what you were born, or what you submitted to, and go take up distaff and wool-basket, twist thread with your thumb; leave wars to men', 12.474–6). The conventional battlefield taunt impugning an opponent's masculinity is somewhat jarring in the mouth of a Centaur. Yet the conventional epic response of the insulted warrior to such a taunt is the immediate vindication of his battle-prowess, and Caeneus too overcomes his opponent in combat while remaining unscathed himself (12.476–93). The outcome attracts the attention of the entire group of Centaurs and provokes them to concentrate their assault on Caeneus (12.495).

Caeneus, however, like Cycnus under the onslaught of Achilles (12.99–101, 131), remains unpierced and unbloodied as his body blunts the Centaurs' weapons (12.496–7; cf. 12.165–7). The Centaurs react to his super-human endurance in battle with the same astonishment (*fecerat attonitos noua res*, 12.498) that the Greek heroes displayed in the face of Nestor's startling assertions about his birth as a woman (12.175–6). Nestor presents Caeneus' ambiguous gender as the focus of the Centaurs' hostility: *'heu dedecus ingens!' | Monychus exclamat . . . 'nos semimari superamur ab hoste!'* (12.498–9, 506; cf. 12.499–503). Ignoring the fact that the Centaurs themselves are only 'half-human' (*semihomines Centauros*, 12.536), Monychus interprets Caeneus' invulnerability as both a reproach and a challenge to their hyper-masculinity.[54] He calls upon his fellows to unite against Caeneus and, by heaping stones and trees on him, to smother him beneath their mass (12.516–17), just as Achilles suffocates Cycnus (12.140–3). The horse-men's united action to overcome Caeneus, however, allows the Lapiths to regroup and return with renewed purpose against the Centaurs (12.532–5).

The fluidity of Caeneus' gender identity is the structural fulcrum of Nestor's lengthy account of the battle of the Centaurs and Lapiths, the framing device of the battle narrative and the focus of both the internal and the external audiences' attention. The Lapith heroes, among whom Caeneus stands out, close ranks to defeat the bestial foe, neither dismissing Caeneus from their number nor disdaining his contribution because of his natal origin. Rather it is the hyper-masculine Centaurs who incur dishonour and disgrace from a woman-man's battle prowess. Yet Caeneus' death (if indeed he dies; it remains uncertain whether he was driven into Tartarus, 12.522–3, or transformed into an *auis unica*, 12.531), retains a shadow of the feminine about it, for not only should real men die by the sword (or spear or even arrow) in epic warfare rather than by suffocation, but suffocation itself is a form of death reserved for the female in the classical imagination.[55] Even the final avian transformation Nestor claims to have seen (12.525–6) retains a trace of the feminine.[56]

A 'natural' hierarchy of gender thus underlies Nestor's narrative much as the gender system informs the structure of the Trojan war in *Metamorphoses* 12. Opening with the outbreak of the Trojan War engendered by the arrival of Helen in Troy (12.1–5), the book closes with the death of Achilles (the symbolic conclusion of the war) at the hands of the unmanly Paris, who is assimilated to (but also contrasted with) the Amazon Penthesilea: *ille igitur tantorum uictor, Achille, | uictus es a timido*

---

[54] On the hyper-masculinity of the Centaurs see DuBois (1982), 31–2.

[55] Loraux (1987), 7–30, and (1995), 88–115; on the shame of hanging, cf. *Od.* 22.462–4.

[56] Loraux (1995), 110 has recently argued, in connection with the comparisons of hanged women to birds in Greek epic and tragedy (Hom. *Od.* 22.468–72; Eur. *Hippol.* 758–63, 828–9), that in Greek myth the suffocated woman 'is like a bird'. Philip Hardie compares (*per litteras*) 'the Euripidean female prayer for escape on wings . . . literalised in the case of the daughters of Anius' (*Met.* 13.667–74). For the correlation between hanging and suffocation, see Loraux (1995), 106.

Graiae raptore maritae! | *at si femineo fuerat tibi Marte cadendum,* | *Thermodontiaca malles cecidisse bipenni* ('And so Achilles, famous conqueror of such great warriors, you were conquered yourself by the timorous thief of a Greek wife! But if you had to fall in feminine warfare, you would have preferred to fall under the Amazon's axe', 12.608–11). Submerged but by no means dismantled in the Ovidian 'Iliad', the battle between the sexes continues to undergird the structure of epic warfare in the *Metamorphoses*.

Lucan retains this gendered framework in war narratives in the *Bellum Ciuile*. In the manner of a historian, Lucan traces the causes of the civil war of 49–45 BCE to the social upheavals of the late Republic with particular attention to the military and political ambitions for supreme power of a small number of prominent Roman aristocrats, especially Caesar (*BC* 1.67–182).[57] It is a critical commonplace that the deformative rhetoric of Lucan's poem ruptures the structures of Roman civic and cosmic order to represent the collapse of the Republic as 'terminal break-down in social relations',[58] but the hierarchy of gender inscribed in the Virgilian structure of war proves peculiarly resistant to 'terminal break-down' even in 'wars more than civil' (*bella . . . plus quam ciuilia, BC* 1.1).

Virgil's thematic interconnection of marriage with war returns in the *Bellum Ciuile* as an image of the fractured social relations that exemplify civil war. Among the *causae* and *belli semina* (1.158–9), Lucan records the death of Julia (1.111–20), daughter of Caesar and wife of Pompey. In the anti-Virgilian logic of the *Bellum Ciuile*, it is her death rather than her marriage that engenders war (*morte tua discussa fides bellumque mouere* | *permissum ducibus,* 1.119–20). As a cause of war, the death of Julia and concomitant dissolution of her marriage with Pompey directly reverses Virgil's representation in the *Aeneid* of the dynastic marriage alliances first of Dido and Aeneas, the cause of the Punic wars, then of Lavinia and Aeneas, the cause of the Italian war. It leaves unchallenged, however, the Virgilian inscription of the gender system in the structure of war. Like Dido, Julia will not rest in death but returns as a warmongering Fury in a dream-vision to Pompey: *diri tum plena horroris imago* | *uisa caput*

---

[57] Cf. 1.183–522; 5.253, 357, 742–4; 7.501–2, 551; etc. On Caesar in the *Bellum Ciuile*, see Masters (1992), 1–10.   [58] Henderson (1988), 135.

maestum per hiantis Iulia terras | tollere et accenso furialis stare sepulchro
('then a ghost full of dread horror appeared, and Julia seemed to lift her
funereal head through the gaping earth and stand in the guise of a Fury
at the kindled funeral pyre', 3.9–11). The conjunction of *diri* and *furialis*
in this description of Julia characterises her as a *Dira* or Fury, and develops a hint already in play in book 1 where her marriage is ill-omened and
funereal (*diro ferales omine taedas*, 1.112), an image that marks her potential to return as a Fury. Moreover her first words ally her with the Furies
and their active preparations for the coming cataclysmic conflict: '*sedibus
Elysiis campoque expulsa piorum | ad Stygias*' inquit '*tenebras manesque
nocentis | post bellum ciuile trahor. uidi ipsa tenentis | Eumenidas, quater-
ent quas uestris lampadas armis*' ('"Driven out of the Elysian fields and
the plain of the blessed after civil war", she said, "I am dragged to the
shadows of the Styx and the guilty ghosts. I myself have seen the Furies
holding the torches which they brandish for your arms",' 3.12–15).[59]

Julia's allusion to the central role of the Eumenides in civil war reso-
nates with several such references to the Furies in Lucan's *Bellum Ciuile*.[60]
Of particular interest is the reference, in the catalogue of prodigies that
terrify the citizenry as Caesar marches inexorably towards Rome, to a
Fury who invests the city (*ingens urbem cingebat Erinys*, 1.572) and
sounds by night the ominous summons of the war-trumpet and the clash
of arms (1.578–80), just as Allecto summons the Italians and Trojans to
war in Latium (*Aen.* 7.511–22). Julia herself assumes the role of the Fury
in book 3, promising to haunt Pompey by night as Caesar will pursue him
by day (*teneat Caesarque dies et Iulia noctes*, 3.27), to take the field herself
against him (*ueniam te bella gerente | in medias acies*, 3.30–1), and to
reclaim him in battle (*bellum | te faciet ciuile meum*, 3.33–4). The central-
ity of the Furies in Lucan's rhetoric of war derives, of course, from the
Aeneid,[61] and alerts us to the multiple Virgilian models for the dream-
vision of Julia to Pompey. To the scenes in which the ghosts of the Trojan
past, Hector and Creusa, appear to Aeneas in book 2, we may add
Allecto's dream-visit to the sleeping Turnus in book 7 and its galvanic
effect on him (7.445–75), which Virgil had already composed as an

---

[59] In Julia's *uidi* (3.14), Lucan may self-referentially signal his debt to the Virgilian
prototype; cf. Hinds (1998), 8–10.
[60] 1.687–8; 4.187; 6.664, 695; 7.169, 778; 9.642; cf. 7.568.
[61] Hardie (1993), 40–8, 62–5.

inversion of Hector's dream-vision to Aeneas, and with which Lucan conflates it. For Pompey's reaction to the dream of Julia is to rush more forcefully[62] to arms (*maior in arma ruit certa cum mente malorum*, 3.37) in combinatorial imitation of Aeneas' rejection of Hector's summons to leave Troy (*arma amens capio; nec sat rationis in armis*, 2.314) and Turnus' acceptance of Allecto's summons to war (*arma amens fremit, arma toro tectisque requirit*, 7.460).[63] The resulting portrait of an active Pompey eager for battle, unparalleled elsewhere in the *Bellum Ciuile*, well exemplifies the continuing force of the female's summons to war.

Like the dead but infernally active Julia, the wives and lovers of the poem's male protagonists are thematically associated with the Furies. Cato's wife Marcia, for example, is introduced into the narrative in conjunction with a funeral (2.327–8). Lucan represents her returning to Cato directly from the burial of her dead husband Hortensius, to whom Cato had given her in marriage after she had borne him three children (2.326–49). Marcia requests a share in the coming conflict as his wife, and the poet portrays their remarriage as 'a barren anti-wedding'[64] that perverts marriage ritual to funerary rite (2.350–80). Remarrying Cato in funereal attire (2.335–6, 365–9), Marcia insists on her right to join him in death (*liceat tumulo scripsisse 'Catonis | Marcia'*, 2.343–4) and in civil war (*da mihi castra sequi: cur tuta in pace relinquar | et sit ciuili propior Cornelia bello?* 2.348–9), the very threats which the Fury-like figure of Julia holds over Pompey in book 3.

Pompey's wife Cornelia also figuratively assumes the role of a Fury after the decisive defeat of the Republican forces at Pharsalia. Even before, however, Marcia and Julia emphasise her potential for affiliation with the Furies, for Marcia aspires to as central a role in the conflict as Cornelia will have (2.348–9), and Julia amplifies this reference by characterising Cornelia as a woman who condemns her husbands to death (*semperque potentis | detrahere in cladem fato damnata maritos*, 3.21–2). After Pharsalia, these hints are realised in Cornelia's self-reproaches for having doomed Pompey to disaster (8.88–105). Imagining that a Fury presides over her marriages (*me pronuba ducit Erinys*, 8.90), she wishes that she had married Caesar (8.88–90) and thereby conferred on him the disas-

---

[62] Denis Feeney notes (*per litteras*) that Julia here 'makes "Magnus" more "himself" for once: "*maior*"!'   [63] On combinatorial allusion, see Hardie (1990a).

[64] Henderson (1988), 135.

trous fortune she credits herself with wreaking on her husbands (8.90–2). Cornelia concludes this train of thought with the reflection that it was in fact she who had consigned the Republican forces to death and disaster in the civil war (8.91–7), in the familiar Virgilian conjunction of the female voice with the summons to war.

Lucan's most fully developed mortal Fury is Cleopatra, the 'disgrace of Egypt and deadly Fury of Latium' (*dedecus Aegypti, Latii feralis Erinys*, 10.59), who seduces Caesar in Egypt and thus threatens to conquer Rome fifteen years before the Virgilian Cleopatra summons the forces of the East to war against Octavian at Actium. Her transgressive sexual activity in seducing Caesar (10.68–9) aligns her with Helen of Troy (10.60–2), and prefigures her transgressive military ambitions on Rome: *terruit illa suo, si fas, Capitolia sistro | et Romana petit inbelli signa Canopo | Caesare captiuo Pharios ductura triumphos* ('she terrified the Capitol with her rattle, if it can be said, and sought Roman standards for unwarlike Canopus, wishing to lead Egyptian triumphs with Caesar captive', 10.63–5). The challenge Cleopatra poses to culturally validated protocols of sexual and military decorum at Rome is laid bare in Lucan's portrait of her perversion of the norms of Roman conquest, which entitle the victorious Roman (male) general to lead in triumphal procession through Rome the (female) personifications of the conquered cities and nations.[65]

The unifying framework that the hierarchy of gender lends the structure of war in the *Aeneid* recurs in the epics of the Flavian period (70–96 CE), which renovate Virgilian usage more urgently and ambitiously than their immediate predecessors in the field. This renewed urgency may be related to the collapse of Julio-Claudian rule and the ensuing civil war which engulfed Rome in the aftermath of Galba's revolt and Nero's suicide at the end of 68 CE. The civil war ended with the investiture of imperial power, late in 69 or early in 70 CE, in the victorious general Vespasian who, like Augustus, promoted a view of himself as the restorer of the state: 'for the whole duration of his rule he held that nothing was more important than first to stabilise the tottering state, which had nearly been destroyed, and then to enhance it' (Suet. *Vesp.* 8.1). Like Augustus,

---

[65] Dio Cass. 51.21.7–8 reports that an effigy of Cleopatra was included in Octavian's triple triumph of 29 BCE, along with her children Alexander Helios and Cleopatra Selene.

Vespasian was the founder of an imperial dynasty, and he meticulously followed his great predecessor's model: he reformed army pay and discipline, initiated the rebuilding of the city of Rome which had been devastated by fire and civil war, renewed the membership of the Senate, streamlined the judicial process, and introduced legislation designed to rein in the 'licentiousness and extravagance' that was perceived to have 'increased without restraint' (*libido atque luxuria coercente nullo inualuerat, Vesp.* 11). Among these measures is recorded legislation that reduced a woman who took another's slave as her lover to a slave herself (*auctor senatui fuit decernendi, ut quae se alieno seruo iunxisset, ancilla haberetur, Vesp.* 11). A similar fascination with Augustan precedent in every area of imperial governance, including that of morality, has been noted in Vespasian's son Domitian,[66] during whose rule (81–96 CE) the epics of Statius, Valerius Flaccus and Silius Italicus, though perhaps begun under Vespasian, first circulated. Assuming the office of censor in perpetuity in 85, Domitian undertook to correct public morals (*suscepta correctione morum, Dom.* 8.3) and is reported to have revived Augustan moral legislation (*Dom.* 8.3, Dio. Cass. 67.2–3), for which he is praised in contemporary court poetry (Mart. *Epigr.* 5.8, 6.2, 6.4, 6.7, 9.6); on two separate occasions he punished Vestal Virgins for sexual misbehaviour (*incestum, Dom.* 8.3–4). The Flavian emperors' architectural, religious, military and legislative programs participate in traditional Roman moralising discourses designed to legitimate their (seizure of imperial) power,[67] and it is in this context that we should interpret the renewed attention in Flavian epic to the gendered structure of war.

Silius' *Punica* demonstrates a particularly close adherence to the Virgilian paradigm. Rejecting the fragmentation of causation in Ovid's war narratives and the historical causation of Lucan's, Silius turns to the *Aeneid* to uncover the origins of the second Punic war in myth. The closing lines of Silius' proem answer the difficult question Virgil addresses to the Muse in the opening lines of the *Aeneid* (*tantaene animis caelestibus irae?* 'can such great anger move heavenly beings?' *Aen.* 1.11; cf. *causas*, 1.8), and signal the Flavian poet's intention to recuperate the

---

[66] Jones (1992), 13; cf. D'Ambra (1993), 36–9.

[67] On the political efficacy of moral legislation, see Edwards (1993), 34–97; on architecture as a rhetoric of social hierarchy, see Edwards (1993), 137–72, and cf. D'Ambra (1993) on the moral context of Domitian's architectural program in the Forum Transitorium.

Aeneid's structure of war: *tantarum causas irarum odiumque perenni | seruatum studio et mandata nepotibus arma | fas aperire mihi superasque recludere mentes* ('the causes of such great anger, the hatred preserved by eternal zeal, the arms bequeathed to descendants, it is right for me to disclose and to unbar the minds of the gods', *Pun.* 1.17–19).

Silius undertakes his inquiry into the origins of the second Punic war in phrasing that borrows extensively from Virgil's procemia, reproducing both the announcement of the origins of the Italian war in book 7 (*Pun.* 1.20 ~ *Aen.* 7.40), and the opening action of the *Aeneid* in his account of Juno's devotion to Carthage and implacable hostility to Rome (*Pun.* 1.21–63 ~ *Aen.* 1.12–80). Juno's instrument for war between Carthage and Rome in the *Punica* is Hannibal, who assumes the goddess' anger at the outset (*iamque deae cunctas sibi belliger induit iras | Hannibal*, 1.38–9) and is animated by it throughout the poem. In *Punica* 4, for example, Juno adopts the form of the eponymous god of Lake Trasimene and appears in a dream to the sleeping Hannibal to urge him to cross the Appennines (4.725–40), thus preparing the way for the Roman defeat at Lake Trasimene in book 5. Again in book 8, after a set-back in Latium, Hannibal is refortified for the conflict by the timely intervention of Juno (*ad spes armorum et furialia uota reducit | praescia Cannarum Iuno*, 8.26–7), who sends the river nymph Anna Perenna, identified by Silius (following Ovid, *F.* 3.523–696) with Dido's sister Anna (8.28–191), to encourage him to engage the Romans at Cannae (8.25–43, 202–241), where the Romans are disastrously defeated (9.278–10.325). After Cannae, however, Silius' Juno evinces an early and unVirgilian willingness to accommodate the designs of Jupiter, for she sends Sleep to overcome Hannibal and prevent him from marching on Rome, in accordance with the will of Jupiter (10.337–71), and later in the poem, acting on the instructions of Jupiter himself, she even dissuades Hannibal from undertaking a second siege of Rome by showing him the divine forces arrayed in defence of the city (12.691–730), in a rehearsal of Venus' appearance to Aeneas during the sack of Troy (*Aen.* 2.589–623).

Silius' debt to Virgil's inscription of the gender system in the structure of war is doubly determined in his characterisation of Hannibal, for he portrays the Carthaginian military leader not only as the tool of Juno but also as the descendant and avenger of Dido. Silius identifies the founder of Hannibal's lineage as Belus (1.72–3), the name of Dido's father in the *Aeneid* (1.621, 729–30), and makes his progenitor Barcas a partisan of

Dido in her flight from Tyre and foundation of Carthage (1.73–6). Hannibal is drawn still further into the fatal recension of the Virgilian Dido, when Silius shows him in a grove sacred to Elissa (as Dido names herself in her deathbed curse of Aeneas, *Aen.* 4.610) swearing an oath by her ghost to harry the Romans by fire and sword in perpetual warfare in a heavily signalled allusion to Dido's call for an avenger to rise from her bones (*Pun.* 1.114–19 ~ *Aen.* 4.625–9).[68] Silius emphasises Hannibal's role as *Dido redux* in the preface to the Carthaginian attack on the Spanish city of Saguntum, in breach of the treaty with Rome, that begins the second Punic war (2.391–4, 446–56). Before the fateful siege, the allies of Carthage present Hannibal with a shield on which is prominently depicted the tragedy of Dido (2.406–25, a summary of *Aeneid* 4) beside Hannibal's siege of Saguntum. As the avatar of both Juno and Dido, Silius' Hannibal is endowed with the transgressive force of the militaristic Virgilian female and simultaneously marked from the outset as the loser in the new epic struggle with Rome, on the model of Juno, Dido, Amata, and the recurrent female opposition to the proto-Roman mission of the *Aeneid.*[69]

As Hannibal invests Saguntum from without (on the shield and in the narrative), so Juno sends Tisiphone to undermine the city from within (2.526–52). Assuming the form of Tiburna, a Saguntine war-widow, the Fury exhorts the Saguntines to mutual slaughter (2.553–79). Prompted by the Fury (*agit abdita Erinnys,* 2.595), they erect a huge funeral pyre and then follow her example in mass carnage (*princeps Tisiphone, lentum indignata parentem,* | *pressit ouans capulum cunctantemque impulit ensem* | *et dirum insonuit Stygio bis terque flagello,* 2.614–16), in a scene that resonates with Lucanian civil war horrors (2.617–95). This passage introduces a note of moral ambivalence concerning the generic affiliation of women with war, for the Saguntines' mass suicide was regarded by the Romans as an exemplary display of the loyalty owed by an ally to Rome. So Silius both praises the Saguntines for their fidelity (in contrast to Punic treachery, 2.654–7), and abhors the carnage with its overtones of civil discord, effectively depicting 'the paradoxical nature of the act, at once glorious and repellent, noble and bestial'.[70] Yet his attribution of praise and blame in this episode also demonstrates an unfaltering com-

---

[68] Hardie (1993), 64–5.

[69] On the female as generic 'loser' in Homeric epic, see Monsacré (1984), 45, 81–4; on the place of the Amazon in this economy, see Henderson (1994), 96–8.

[70] Feeney (1991), 308.

mitment to the 'natural' hierarchy of gender in the structure of Roman epic warfare, for the glorious achievement of the Saguntines is inspired by Hercules, who sends Loyalty to fortify the citizens out of concern for the city he founded (2.475–525), while their unheroic mutual slaughter is provoked by Tisiphone (disguised as Tiburna), acting on Juno's instructions.

In contrast to Silius, whose *Punica* pits a feminised foreign enemy against Roman male order, Statius and Valerius Flaccus thematise conflict between the sexes in civil war narratives. Intrafamilial conflict and civil war pervade Valerius' *Argonautica*, which opens with Pelias enjoining upon his nephew Jason the quest for the golden fleece because there are no wars in Greece to which he can be sent (1.33–4; cf. 5.495–7). The shadow of war, and especially civil war, looms large over the journey of the Argonauts: at Cyzicus they inadvertently do battle with their erstwhile hosts (3.15–458); in Colchis they find a civil war under way (3.487–508, 5.265–6.760); internecine conflict erupts among the 'Sown Men' (7.607–43); the fleece itself hangs in a grove sacred to the war-god Mars (1.528–9, 5.228–30); the Colchians under Absyrtus pursue the Argonauts to try to recover the fleece (8.259–467). Paradoxically, the only war in which the Argonauts do not participate is the first fully narrated conflict in the poem, the Lemnian massacre which occurs just before the Argonauts arrive on the island of Lemnos (2.101–310).

Precisely because the Argonauts do not participate in the Lemnian conflict, the episode invites interpretation as a commentary on the economy of war in the *Argonautica*. The Lemnian episode shows significant points of contact with the Argonautic project, most obviously in the interconnection of war with sea-travel. The Lemnian men make use of the technology of ship-building and sea-faring to wage a long war in Thrace (2.107–14), much as the Argonauts' voyage provides them with the opportunity to engage in wars throughout the Mediterranean and the Black Seas. The Lemnian men's spoils of war are herds and female slaves (2.111–14), rewards which resonate symbolically with the twin prizes, the fleece and Medea, of which Jason will despoil the Colchians. On Lemnos, however, the absence of the men undermines the social order and results in intrafamilial conflict, just as in Thessaly the absence of Jason gives Pelias the opportunity to kill the hero's parents Aeson and Alcimede. Besides the thematic interconnections between the Lemnians' war in Thrace and the Argonauts' journey, the massacre on Lemnos foreshadows the civil war in which Jason and the

Argonauts are embroiled at Colchis, and anticipates their night battle at Cyzicus. Finally, Jason's dalliance with Hypsipyle after civil war on Lemnos rehearses his acquisition of a wife after civil war at Colchis. The Lemnian episode thus furnishes an exemplary model of the structure of war in the *Argonautica*.

The Lemnian massacre thematically pairs conflict between the sexes with civil war, and borrows extensively from the *Aeneid* in the process.[71] Venus inaugurates the conflict on Lemnos (*struit illa nefas Lemnoque merenti | exitium furiale mouet*, 2.101–2). Just as Juno instigated civil conflict thematised as conflict between the sexes among the Trojans in *Aeneid* 5 through Iris and among the Italians in *Aeneid* 7 through Allecto, so in Valerius' *Argonautica* Venus uses another Virgilian female, *Fama*, to spur the Lemnian women to civil war by spreading rumours that the Lemnian men, enslaved by luxury and lust (2.131–2; cf. *Aen.* 4.193–4), intend to turn their wives out of their homes and set Thracian captives in their places (2.115–34). Disguising herself as Neaera *Fama* passes among the Lemnian women, sowing dissension (2.135–61) so effectively that they flee their houses and marriages (2.162–73, on the model of the Italian women in *Aeneid* 7). As they throng the city to bewail the perfidy of their husbands, the disguised Venus proposes that they slaughter their husbands that evening (2.174–84), a suggestion meeting with an enthusiastic reception (2.184–7) reminiscent of the Trojan women's response in *Aeneid* 5 to Iris-Beroe's proposal to fire the ships (*Arg.* 2.186 ~ *Aen.* 5.643). When their husbands return, the Lemnian women feign celebration (2.188–9) as Deiphobus describes Helen doing on the night of the sack of Troy (*Aen.* 6.517–9).

That night Venus returns in the guise of a Fury and summons the women to slaughter (2.196–215). The central role of the Furies in the Latin epic war narrative is the single most commonly rehearsed Virgilian motif, but Valerius innovates in his reuse of the commonplace by applying it to Venus from the outset (*pinum . . . sonantem | uirginibus Stygiis nigramque simillima pallam*, 2.105–6), in a pointed allusion to the structural parallel between Venus' dispatch of Cupid to manipulate Dido in *Aeneid* 1 and Juno's dispatch of Allecto to manipulate Amata in *Aeneid* 7.[72] In a further innovation, the Lemnian women are collectively

---

[71] On Valerius' debts to Virgil in this passage, see Hardie (1990a), 5–9; and Hardie (1993), 43–4.

[72] On the structural parallel in the *Aeneid*, see Lyne (1987), 13–27; on Valerius' combinatorial allusion, see Hardie (1990a).

compared, in their eagerness to murder their husbands, to the Fury Tisiphone punishing sinners in the underworld (2.190–5), another allusion to the *Aeneid* (6.548–72). When the slaughter begins, moreover, the women's murderous attack on their menfolk is compared to the onslaught of the Furies and Bellona in battle (*uelut agmina cernant | Eumenidum ferrumue super Bellona coruscet. | hoc soror, hoc coniunx, propiorque hoc nata parensque | saeua ualet*, 2.227–30). The Furies who elsewhere in the poem summon men into conflict on the Virgilian model of war (1.817, 3.214, 3.520, 4.13, 6.403) are on Lemnos physically embodied in the women who instigate the worst kind of insurrection against the political order of the state, a conflict that overturns the natural hierarchy of gender and moves the poet to intervene directly in his narrative to comment on the magnitude of the women's crime (2.216–19). The Lemnian women's slaughter of their menfolk takes to its (ideo)logical limit the reversal of social order implicit in civil war and reveals at every point the pressure of the gendered structure of war at play in the *Aeneid.*

Valerius' unfinished poem, however, can match neither Silius' *Punica* nor Statius' *Thebaid* in the extent and coherence of its affiliation of woman with war. Statius achieves the most fully integrated and innovative reuse of the Virgilian imbrication of the gender system in the structure of war in Flavian epic. Like all Roman epicists after Virgil, he assigns the Furies a central role in his epic war narrative. The poem opens with a description of Oedipus' life-in-death after the discovery of his incestuous marriage and parricide (1.46–55). The blind former king lurks in the recesses of the palace and shuns contact with all, his only company the *Dirae* who have taken up residence in his breast (*illum . . . adsiduis circumuolat alis | saeua dies animi, scelerumque in pectore Dirae*, 1.51–2). Under their tutelage it is no surprise that he prays to the Fury Tisiphone rather than the Olympian gods to accomplish his curse against his sons (1.53–88). The Furies are thereby unleashed to instigate fratricidal conflict (*fraternas acies*, 1.1) and civil war at Thebes, a role they have played many times in Thebes' history, beginning with the civil war among the Spartoi, born from the earth in which Cadmus sows the teeth of the dead serpent (*quis funera Cadmi | nesciat et totiens excitam a sedibus imis | Eumenidum bellasse aciem*, 1.227–9). Tisiphone immediately leaves Hades for Thebes, heading directly to the palace where she enmeshes the brothers in conflict (*indomitos praeceps discordia fratres | asperat*, 1.137–8). Losing Thebes to Eteocles by lot, Polynices travels in exile to

Argos where he acquires a wife, a brother-in-law, and an Argive force he can deploy against Thebes.

Statius delays the war for five books, but when the Argive forces arrive at Thebes the Fury duly initiates war and accomplishes Oedipus' curse. Investing the massed troops, Tisiphone is at first unable to incite hostilities (7.466–9) for Jocasta temporarily succeeds in averting an engagement (7.470–534). Her success cannot last, however, as Statius signals in the very comparison that introduces her onto the battlefield, rushing out 'like the most ancient of the Furies', with filthy hair and bloody cheeks, holding in arms black with bruises an olive-branch that should betoken peace but is bound with funereal skeins (*ecce truces oculos sordentibus obsita canis | exangues Iocasta genas et bracchia planctu | nigra ferens ramumque oleae cum uelleris atri | nexibus, Eumenidum uelut antiquissima*, 7.474–7; cf. *luctu furiata*, 7.489). In her speech, Jocasta names herself the impious mother of the war (*impia belli | mater*, 7.483–4), a formulation that hardly inspires confidence in her ability to promote a peaceful settlement at this juncture. As she recognises, in fact, her marriage and motherhood align her with the Furies in promoting the conflict (*nupsi equidem peperique nefas*, 7.514). Her intervention, although successful for a short period, ultimately proves ineffectual against the onslaught of the Fury, who maddens twin tigers regarded with religious awe at Thebes and thereby engenders the first skirmish (*fera tempus Erinys | arripit et primae molitur semina pugnae*, 7.562–3). Inflamed by the Fury (*Eumenis in furias . . . impulit*, 7.580–1), they attack Amphiaraus' charioteer only to be tracked and killed by Aconteus as war erupts before the walls of Thebes (7.608–31).

In addition to maintaining a central role for the Furies in engendering conflict, Statius revives the Virgilian motif of the wife who destines her husband to war.[73] On the day of the double wedding at Argos of Adrastus' daughters Argia and Deipyle to Polynices and Tydeus, *Fama* announces marriage to the cities allied with Argos (2.201–7) but war to

---

[73] Valerius also seems to have planned to reuse this motif in the *Argonautica*. Just before book 8 breaks off, the Argonauts reproach Jason for enmeshing them in conflict with the Colchians because of Medea (8.385–8), who assumes the role of Helen in the Trojan war or Lavinia in the Italian war. There may be a hint of this earlier in the references to the participation of Medea's Albanian fiancé in the civil war at Colchis because of the prospective marriage alliance (3.495–7, 5.256–8, 459–60, 6.42–7, 270–8).

Thebes (*hospitia et thalamos et foedera regni | permixtumque genus . . . et iam bella canit*, 2.211–13). Part of Argia's trousseau is the necklace of Harmonia (2.265–305), a deadly device (*infaustos . . . | ornatus . . . dirumque monile | Harmoniae. longa est series sed nota malorum*, 2.265–7) fashioned by the Cyclopes and the Telchines on Vulcan's instructions as a gift for the daughter of his wife Venus by her lover Mars (2.269–76), on the occasion of her marriage to the founder of Thebes, Cadmus. On the necklace is engraved a series of ill-omened figures (including the Gorgons, the Hesperides, and Tisiphone), and the whole piece is lavishly smeared with poisons (2.277–85).[74] The necklace symbolises strife itself: *non hoc Pasithea blandarum prima sororum, | non Decor Idaliusque puer, sed Luctus et Irae | et Dolor et tota pressit Discordia dextra* (2.286–8). By wearing the necklace Argia is drawn into the series of intrafamilial conflicts that recurs in every generation (and between every generation) in the House of Cadmus. Moreover, the necklace enmeshes another hero in the conflict between Polynices and Eteocles, for when Amphiaraus' wife sees it she determines to acquire it (2.299–305) and commits her husband to joining the expedition in return for the necklace (4.59–62, 187–213; cf. 8.104–5, 120–2). By marrying Polynices, Argia also becomes privy to his desire for war with his brother (2.319–62), and so it is she who overcomes her father's reluctance to send the Seven to war against Thebes (3.678–721). Book 4 opens with the formal outbreak of war, in which Statius' Bellona outdoes her Virgilian counterpart Juno (who merely breaks open the Gates of War, 7.620–2), by hurling the fetial spear all the way from Argos to Thebes (4.5–8).

Statius also exploits Virgil's thematic pairing of conflict between the sexes with civil war in his account of the Lemnian massacre, narrated by Hypsipyle to the Argive leaders (5.29–498). As in Valerius' *Argonautica*, to which it may allude, Statius' account of the Lemnian women's slaughter of their menfolk invites interpretation as a commentary on the structure of war in the *Thebaid* as a whole.[75] Hypsipyle's account begins with the conventional reference to the central role of the Furies in conflict, and the assurance that the women's rebellion against the hierarchy of gender merits the most severe condemnation (*Furias et Lemnon et artis | arma*

---

[74] The poisonous necklace recalls the necklace into which Allecto's snake is transformed as it encircles and maddens Amata at *Aen.* 7.351–5.

[75] Götting (1969), 63–86; Vessey (1970), and (1973), 170–87; Aricò (1991); John Henderson (1991), 56.

inserta toris debellatosque pudendo | ense mares; redit ecce nefas et frigida cordi | Eumenis, 5.30–3). Hypsipyle identifies Venus (5.58–69, 157–8, 303) and Polyxo (5.90–142) as the instigators of the women's violence: Venus provokes the men to prefer war in Thrace to their marriages on Lemnos (5.75–89) and, in the absence of the men, Polyxo challenges the Lemnian women to assume the conventionally male prerogatives of militarism and government (5.97–103). Similes link Polyxo and the Lemnians to the militant and militaristic women of myth (a Maenad, 5.92–4; Procne, 5.120–2; the Amazons, 5.144–6). With the convenient return of the Lemnian men, therefore, each woman is prompted by her own Fury (*cuncto sua regnat Erinys | pectore*, 5.202–3) to embark on a slaughter that pits family member against family member and overturns the 'natural' hierarchy of the sexes (5.200–39). The women's violence survives the slaughter of their men, and leads them to try to oppose the landing of the Argonauts (5.347–60) before Venus cools their battle-lust (5.445–6). In the topsy-turvy world of Lemnos, where all order is overwhelmed once the hierarchy of gender has been overturned, Hypsipyle's rescue of her father can only be represented as a crime (5.486–92) for which she pays at Nemea with the death of Opheltes (*exsolui tibi, Lemne, nefas*, 5.628).

Throughout the *Thebaid*, Statius rehearses Virgil's inscription of gender in the economy of war while remaining sensitive to the *Aeneid*'s final failure to sustain the hierarchy of gender within the structure of war. The most consistent advocate of peaceful settlement is the Argive king Adrastus, Polynices' father-in-law and the literary descendant of Latinus. Adrastus demonstrates a commitment to peace from the outset when he reconciles the quarrelling Polynices and Tydeus on their first meeting (1.467–81), and he repeatedly attempts to reconcile Polynices and Eteocles – through the embassy of Tydeus (2.364–74), counsel (3.386–93) and consultation of the gods (3.442–59), support of Jocasta's doomed intervention on the battlefield before the outbreak of hostilities (7.537–8), and mediation before the brothers' climactic duel (11.110–11, 196–7, 426–43). Tydeus and Amphiaraus give subsidiary and inconsistent support to Adrastus at Argos. At Thebes, by contrast, the Fury-like Jocasta receives support from an unusually pacific pair of women, her daughters Antigone and Ismene (7.534–7, 11.354–82), although it is Menœceus whom the poet identifies as the author of Theban peace (*auctorem pacis*, 10.684).

The figure who imposes a lasting settlement on Thebes and Argos in the final book of the poem, however, is neither Theban nor Argive but Athenian, the hero Theseus. His qualifications for this role are twofold. He has just returned from war with the Amazons (*prope namque et Thesea fama est | Thermodontiaco laetum remeare triumpho*, 12.163–4) whom he has utterly routed, the definitive evidence lying in his translation of their leader Hippolyte from the battlefield to his bed (12.519–39). In a neat reversal of the disorder that reigned on the island of Lemnos, Theseus' victory over the Amazons restores the order of the cosmos by reinstating the 'natural' hierarchy of gender. By mastering those militant women, Theseus symbolically earns the authority to impose settlement in the world of the *Thebaid*.[76] Moreover, he is explicitly invited by the suppliant Argive women to attack Thebes and restore order to Greece by allowing them to bury their dead (12.540–88). Acting on Argia's instructions (12.196–204), and protected by Juno (12.464–518), the Argive women surround the altar of Clemency at Athens and entreat Theseus to march on Thebes, where Creon refuses to allow the Argive dead burial. Addressing Theseus as a warrior (*belliger Aegide*, 12.546), the Argive women invite him to prove his reputation for military prowess and avenge their slain husbands (12.570–2). Statius brilliantly encapsulates Theseus' dual function as war-commander and peace-officer in the report of his demands to Thebes: *ille quidem ramis insontis oliuae | pacificus, sed bella ciet bellumque minatur, | grande fremens* ('peacemaker indeed with branches of harmless olive, but he provokes battles and threatens war, raging mightily', 12.682–4).

Creon, the new Theban ruler, is of course inspired by the Furies to choose war rather than permit the slain Argives to be buried (*Eumenidas subitas flentemque Menoecea cernit*, 12.696). Accordingly, he is duly dispatched to the underworld by Theseus (12.774–88), in a scene that rehearses Aeneas' killing of Turnus at the end of the *Aeneid*. The *Thebaid* closes not with Creon's death on the battlefield, however, but with a gesture to reconciliation as the Argive women set about burying their dead (12.789–809). Yet the lamentation of the women is likened to the clamour of the Maenads summoning their ranks to war, a finale that pointedly emphasises the tenacious interconnection of gender, war, and the engendering of war in Roman epic: *ecce per aduersas Dircaei uerticis umbras | femineus quatit astra fragor, matresque Pelasgae | decurrunt:*

---

[76] Cf. DuBois (1982), 66.

quales Bacchea ad bella uocatae | Thyiades amentes, magnum quas poscere credas | aut fecisse nefas ('lo the roar of the women moving through the shadows of Mt. Dirce shook the stars, and the Greek mothers ran down, like the frenzied Maenads summoned to Dionysiac wars, whom you might believe were demanding, or had accomplished, a great crime', 12.789–93). Statius' closing lines hint that no occasion is immune from women's violent summons to war.[77]

[77] Cf. Huston (1986).

Over her dead body[1]

The death of a beautiful woman is, unquestionably, the most poetical topic
in the world.

(Edgar Allan Poe, 'The Philosophy of Composition')

In Greco-Roman mythology and legend, the death of a beautiful woman
often serves as the prelude or postlude to war.[2] Thus the Greek expedition to Troy departs from Aulis only after the sacrifice of Iphigenia, the
daughter of the commander-in-chief. When the Greek army is similarly
becalmed in Thrace after the Trojan war, the sacrifice of Polyxena
appeases the wrath of Achilles' ghost and secures the Greek ships favour-
able winds for the homeward journey. Although Homeric epic takes as its
primary subject the Trojan war and its aftermath, the poems ignore the
deaths of these maidens in their focus on male death and heroism.[3] This
omission is striking since we know that two of the Cyclic epics included
the deaths of Iphigenia (*Cypria*) and Polyxena (*Iliupersis*; cf. *Cypria* fr.
27).[4] Although the motif gained prominence in fifth-century Athenian

---

[1] In a provocative study with this title, Bronfen (1992) discusses the thematic connections of 'death, femininity and the aesthetic' (her subtitle) in nineteenth-century
European literature and art. Her focus precludes sustained exploration of the intersection of these themes in earlier European artistic traditions.

[2] Burkert (1979), 72–6, and (1983), 64–7; Dowden (1989).

[3] Cf. Heuzé (1985), 130. On (male) death in the *Iliad*, see Griffin (1980), 81–143; Schein
(1984), 67–8; Vernant (1991); on (male) death in the *Odyssey*, see Nagler (1990).

[4] Cf. the death of Penthesilea, narrated in the *Aethiopis.*

drama,[5] it never seems to have achieved canonical status in Greek epic. In the Hellenistic period Callimachus set a woman's unheroic death at the centre of his *Hecale* but his innovation does not seem to have inspired imitation, if Apollonius' contemporary composition of an *Argonautica* (despite the prominence of Medea in books 3 and 4) and a host of titles of works now vanished offer a reliable index of the state of Hellenistic Greek epic.[6]

In Roman epic, by contrast, dead and dying women assume a new thematic and aesthetic prominence,[7] for the beautiful female corpse possesses an intrinsic importance in Roman political myths of war and city foundation, the pre-eminent subjects of epic at Rome. At crucial moments in the legendary history of Rome the rape and death of a woman set in motion events leading to the establishment of political institutions central to the Roman state.[8] Lucretia, for example, raped by the tyrannical son of the Etruscan king of Rome, commits suicide in the presence of her kinsmen who avenge her death by inciting the populace to overthrow the Etruscan monarchy and establish a Republican form of government (Livy 1.57–9). Livy links the death of Lucretia to that of the plebeian Verginia (3.44), who escapes the sexual assault of the tyrannical decemvir Appius because her father murders her; he then incites a public outcry against Appius' arrogance which leads to the overthrow of the Decemvirate, the re-establishment of the Tribunate and the resumption of the normal workings of the political institutions of the Republic (3.44–58). Earlier in the city's history the rape of the Sabine women, which almost leads to the women's death when they intervene on the battlefield to separate the army of their Roman husbands from that of their Sabine fathers and brothers (1.13.1–2), ensures Rome's existence beyond the first generation and underwrites the union of Romans and

---

[5] Aesch. *Ag.* 122–248; Eur. *Alc.*, *Hec.*, *Hel.*, *I.A.*, *I.T.*, *Tro.*, *Med.* 1125–1203, *Supp.* 980–1113. Euripides' interest in the theme is discussed by Rabinowitz (1993), who argues that Euripidean tragedy founds the exchange mechanisms of Greek society (marriage, sacrifice, *xenia*) on violence against the female body; cf. Foley (1982) and Wilkins (1990), 190. [6] Hainsworth (1991), 57–75.

[7] This development may be connected with the Roman epicists' well-documented interest in Athenian tragic models, with close interplay between Latin epic and Euripidean tragedy from the start, since Ennius composed Euripidean tragedy: see Jocelyn (1967).

[8] See Donaldson (1982); Hemker (1985), 41–7; Stehle (1989); Joplin (1990); Joshel (1992); and cf. Kahn (1991). Cf. Kraus (1991) on Fabia Minor (Livy 6.34.5–35.1).

Sabines into a single people whom Romulus organises into thirty wards named after the raped women (1.13.6–7). The Sabine women's rape and narrow escape from death find an analogue on the Roman side in the betrayal of the city to the Sabines by Tarpeia, variously identified as the daughter of the Roman commander and a Vestal Virgin.[9] Although Livy (1.11.6) and Plutarch (*Rom.* 17.2–3) attribute her treachery to greed, others ascribe it to love for the enemy commander.[10] In both versions Tarpeia is killed by the very enemy whom she helps, and the site of her treachery and death, the Capitoline citadel (from which criminals were thrown to their death in the historical period), is commemorated as the 'Tarpeian rock'.[11]

Among these figures we may include Ilia, or Rhea Silvia as Livy calls her, who is raped by the war-god Mars and bears the twins Romulus and Remus, the eponymous founders of Rome (1.4.4–8). Her story has garnered relatively little attention, perhaps because Livy's treatment is so brief.[12] The historian passes swiftly over the Vestal's claim to have been raped by a god (which he discredits), devoting his narrative instead to the birth of the twins Romulus and Remus, and their upbringing and education (1.3.11–4.8). Livy entirely omits the Vestal's death by drowning in the Tiber and subsequent 'marriage' to the river: after he records her imprisonment she vanishes from his narrative altogether. Yet she stands at the very head of the legendary history of Rome and inaugurates the sequence of women raped and killed in the course of the establishment of the city and its political institutions. She is thus a paradigmatic figure, central not merely to the elaboration of a Livian topos, but also to the elaboration of a Roman ideology of gender relations, for her rape and death received canonical treatment in the first book of Ennius' *Annales*, an account which influenced all subsequent versions of her tale, including Livy's.[13]

This chapter explores the representation of female death in Latin epic, not to suggest that it replaces male heroism and death as the focus of the

---

[9] Tarpeia as a daughter of the Roman commander: Livy 1.11.6, Plu. *Rom.* 17.2; Tarpeia as a Vestal Virgin: Var. *Ling.* 5.41; Prop. 4.4.17–18; Val. Max. 9.6.1; and cf. Livy 1.11.6, *uirginem.*   [10] Prop. 4.4.19–92; Simylus *ap.* Plu. *Rom.* 18.5.

[11] Var. *Ling.* 5.41; Prop. 4.4.93; Dion. Hal. 3.69.4; Plu. *Rom.* 18.1.

[12] Cf. Hemker (1985), 41; Joplin (1990), 58–9.

[13] Other narrative accounts of the rape of Ilia include Ov. *Am.* 3.6.45–82, *F.* 3.11–52; Dion. Hal. 1.77.2; Conon, 48 *FGH* I p. 209; *Origo gentis Romanae* 20.1.

genre, but to establish the intersection of 'death, femininity and the aesthetic' in this literature.[14] Female death is pervasively sexualised in Latin epic, and I contend that the violence and sexuality of the male heroes of epic are consistently displaced onto the female body, which is represented as the site where sexuality and violence coincide.[15] I argue that the sight of a beautiful female corpse often serves as the prelude to the action of Roman epic poetry, and that the political order which emerges at the close of the poem, whether contested or confirmed, is established over her dead body. The objectification of the female inherent in this sight founds the subjectivity of the epic hero (and his readers) as political agents. Female death assumes a new importance in Latin epic at least in part because it entails beneficial consequences for the political community of male survivors.

As Rome's first hexameter-epic poet, Ennius carefully fashioned in the *Annales* a history of Rome from its foundation to his own day, bearing witness to the institutions that contributed to Rome's military success and imperial expansion as well as asserting his own poetic achievement in instituting hexameter epic at Rome. We may expect Ennius to be at his most self-conscious in his account of Ilia's rape by Mars, for from this rape is born the city of Rome, the subject of his poem.[16] Ennius narrates the rape of the Vestal in the form of a dream in which the maiden is dragged along a river bank by a beautiful man who vanishes without explanation (38–9); confused and disoriented (40–2), she hears the disembodied voice of her father Aeneas who comforts her and then vanishes (43–50).[17] The incorporeality of the male characters (which, to be sure, befits figures appearing in a dream) contrasts strikingly with Ennius' fully-fleshed portrait of Ilia. She opens her account of the dream by lamenting that her body seems bereft of strength (*uires, corpus,* 37), but represents herself in her dream slowly tracking her half-sister, although unsure of her footing (*pedem,* 42) and 'unable to reach' her (*corde capessere,* 42).[18] Ilia's gaze (*conspectum,* 47) fails to detect her father (although

---

[14] On the themes of male heroism and death in Latin epic, see Heuzé (1985); and Hardie (1993), 3–11.

[15] This tendency finds further expression in the displacement of sexualised violence onto the feminised body of the young hero: cf. Fowler (1987), and Oliensis (1997).

[16] Cf. Dominik (1993), 42; Krevans (1993), 265 n. 28; Connors (1994), 100–7.

[17] On Ennius' debt to tragic models in Ilia's dream, see Krevans (1993).

[18] Skutsch (1985), 199.

she has heard his words), to her heartfelt disappointment (*corde cupitus*, 47). Neither her hands raised to the heavens (*manus*, 48), nor her tears (*lacrumans*, 49) provoke any further response. The passage invests Ilia with a striking materiality of body (tears, hands, heart, foot, life, strength, body), while denying a comparable physicality to either her divine rapist or her father. Indeed, embodiment in this passage is exclusively reserved for the female characters, as Ennius also endows Ilia's aged nurse with 'shaking limbs' (*tremulis . . . artubus*, 34).

I argued in chapter 3 that the physical setting of the *locus amoenus* is closely associated in the Ennian narrative with Ilia's body and we may extend that conclusion here by considering the gendered distribution of grammatical subjects and objects in the passage. Mars, Aeneas, and Amulius are represented as agents acting upon an objectified Ilia (*Ann.* 38–9, 43–5 Sk.). Mars is the subject of the verb *raptare* of which Ilia is the grammatical object *me* (38), in the phrase which both alludes to and occludes Mars' sexual assault of Ilia. His sexual possession of Ilia prefigures her son's political possession of the landscape in which she will be immersed. Aeneas addresses Ilia (43) but neither waits to hear her response nor appears to her anxious gaze (46–9), while the speech he addresses to her casts her as the unwilling recipient of the troubles which she must endure (44–5) and the destiny which awaits her. The evidence is admittedly scanty, but it appears that Ennius dealt with this part of the story by depicting Ilia's death by drowning as analogous to marriage with the river.[19] Porphyrio, commenting on Horace *C.* 1.2.18, remarks that 'according to Ennius Ilia was hurled into the river Tiber on the order of Amulius, king of the Albans, and was joined in marriage with Antemnian Anio',[20] in a summary that casts Ilia as the subject of two grammatically passive verbs (*praecipitata, iuncta est*). Two fragmentary lines of the *Annales* seem to belong to this part of Ilia's story: a half-line quoted by Servius, discussing *Aen.* 3.333, shows Ilia duly delivered for marriage (*at Ilia reddita nuptum*, 56), while another line may relate the accomplishment of Amulius' orders (*haec ecfatus, ibique latrones dicta facessunt*, 'he said this and the brigands thereupon fulfilled his orders', 57).

This putative redefinition of death as marriage parallels the treatment

---

[19] On Ennius' use of Athenian tragic models, see Skutsch (1985), 193–201; on Ennius' debt to the Homeric Tyro, see Dominik (1993), 42, and Connors (1994), 102–4. On the woman's death as an ideological requirement following upon her rape, see Joshel (1992).   [20] (*Ann.* I fr. xxxix Sk.).

of Ilia's rape as a dream, and finds expression on the level of form in the 'remarkable delicacy'[21] of the diction Ennius employs throughout the passage, and especially in the description of the rape itself (*nam me uisus homo pulcer per amoena salicta | et ripas raptare locosque nouos*, 'for a handsome man seemed to drag me through pleasant willow-groves, river-banks and new places' 38–9). The Ennian Ilia gestures towards rape by metaphor (*locos nouos*) and metonymy (*raptare*).[22] Both *rapto* and *rapio* have a basic sense of 'drag off into captivity' and imply that the act is carried out against the will of the victim; but the act of violence need not be sexual. The sympathetic representation of Ilia's subsequent disorientation and distress (39–50) confirms the implications of violence and unwillingness, though Ennius suppresses any reference to specifically sexual violence.[23] We may relate this omission to a tendency Amy Richlin has recently observed in connection with the rapes in Ovid's *Metamorphoses*: 'Ovid's rapes are not sexually explicit. But no such limits hamper the poem's use of violence, which sometimes stands in for the sexual.'[24] Ennius' use of the verb *raptare* 'gestures towards' or 'figures' the rape; it stands in for the rape but does not confront the rape directly. In this way, Ennius engages in what the editors of a collection of essays entitled *Rape and Representation* have called 'the rhetoric of elision'.[25]

Just such a rhetoric of elision can be discerned in Ennius' deployment of erotic vocabulary throughout Ilia's account of her dream.[26] Ilia addresses her half-sister not by name but in a periphrasis (*Eurydica prognata, pater quam noster amauit*, 'daughter of Eurydice, whom our father loved', 36) which recalls the love of Aeneas for his first wife and thereby evokes Ilia's love for her half-sibling. Ilia acknowledges her desire for her half-sister's comfort in her dream in the phrase *corde capessere* (42), which Skutsch discusses at some length. He suggests translating 'to reach you',[27] but observes that the phrase seems to convey the sense of *cupitam capessere*, and compares Ilia's expression of desire for her father's comfort in the words *corde cupitus* (47). Both phrases admit an undercurrent of desire to the narrative, especially since Ilia continues to call for Aeneas with a seductive voice after he stops speaking (*blanda uoce*, 49).

[21] Skutsch (1985), 198.
[22] For the metonymy, see Adams (1982), 175; cf. Connors (1994), 101.
[23] Cf. Connors (1994), 104–5.   [24] Richlin (1992a), 162.
[25] Higgins and Silver (1991), 5–6.   [26] Cf. Krevans (1993), 261; Connors (1994), 105.
[27] Skutsch (1985), 199.

Ilia's expressions of affection and desire for her father and sister can be read as constituting 'a socially constrained displacement of [her] desires for the *pulcer homo*';[28] but the same rhetorical strategy that displaces Ilia's desire for Mars from the *pulcer homo* on to her family also deflects responsibility for sexual violence, sexuality and sexual desire from Mars back on to Ilia.

Although reconstruction of the role of Mars in Ennius' narrative must remain uncertain, the surviving fragments reveal if not an Ennian focus on Ilia, at least a conscious interest in Ilia on the part of Ennius' readers.[29] Mars' role in the proceedings is marginal in the extant fragments of the Ennian narrative: unnamed, he receives only a line and a half in Ilia's report of her dream (38–9). In allowing Ilia to narrate the dream that represents the rape, then, Ennius reaffirms the patriarchal structures that he encodes in her account, for the focalisation of the rape through the speaking Ilia invites us to locate the site of sexuality exclusively in the body of the female. The fragments of Ennius' *Annales* treating the story of Ilia reveal considerable sympathy for her; but at the same time they inscribe her in an ideological system that associates the female with the body, the body with sexuality, and sexuality with death. This logic culminates in the assimilation of the raped woman's body to the ground of the state, when the site of the future city of Rome – the dreamscape of Ilia's sexual initiation – becomes the site of her death. Ennius' triumphal narrative of the rise of Rome is predicated on the death of Ilia and the concomitant closure of the narrative of Ilia. Incorporated into the ground of the state, Ilia's fecund body ensures not only the immediate safety of her sons but also the future prosperity of Rome and the continuation of Ennius' narrative.

The influence of the *Annales* is visible throughout *De Rerum Natura*, and Lucretius explicitly acknowledges a debt to Ennian epic early in the poem (1.117–26). Homage to Ennius follows directly upon a passage relating the sacrifice of Iphigenia that reveals numerous points of contact with Ennius' treatment of Ilia's rape and death (and Euripides' treatment

---

[28] Catherine Connors (*per litteras*).

[29] Evidence for Ennius' Ilia is preserved in fragments (quoted by Macrobius, Cicero, Varro, Servius, Tertullian, Nonius, Charisius and Fronto), testimonia (of Porphyrio on Hor. *C.* 1.2.18 and Servius on Virg. *Aen.* 8.630), and imitations (by Livy, 1.3.10–4.3; Horace, *C.* 1.2.17–20, 3.2.32–3, 3.9.8; and Ovid, *Am.* 3.6.45–82). Ovid singles out the Ilia story for comment on the *Annales* at *Tr.* 2.259–60.

of Iphigenia at Aulis, adapted by Ennius in his *Iphigenia*.[30] Discussion of 'woman' in *De Rerum Natura* has traditionally focused on the generative body, but Georgia Nugent has recently maintained, to the contrary, that Lucretius pervasively associates the female with death. In this connection she has drawn attention to the Epicurean poet's tendency to emphasise woman's corporeality and her link with dirt, disease and death in passages as diverse as the diatribe against love (4.1058–1287) and the discussion of earthquakes (6.535–607).[31] The sacrifice of Iphigenia which the poet treats as paradigmatic of the evils of *religio* is an early example of this nexus of themes (which is not discussed by Nugent). Lucretius opens the passage with a graphic description of the maiden's blood defiling Diana's altar: *Aulide quo pacto Triuiai uirginis aram | Iphianassai turparunt sanguine foede | ductores Danaum delecti, prima uirorum* ('at Aulis, for instance, the chosen leaders of the Greeks, first among men, foully stained the altar of the maiden Diana with Iphigenia's blood', 1.84–6).[32] In a tightly-focused four-word hexameter (1.85), the poet interweaves Iphigenia's blood with a verb and adverb connoting staining and pollution, in order to underline the sacrilegious impiety of her sacrifice. Although the Greek leaders are responsible for this impiety, it is the sacrificial victim whose blood contaminates the sacred altar and who is thereby constituted as 'a messy, bloody body'.[33]

In his portrait of Iphigenia, Lucretius draws on Greek tragic representations of Agamemnon's daughter as bride of death.[34] With her hair encircled by a fillet hanging down over both cheeks, Iphigenia is ritually prepared for both marriage and sacrifice (*cui simul infula uirgineos circumdata comptus | ex utraque pari malarum parte profusast*, 1.87–8). This description of Iphigenia's hairstyle recalls the *sex crines*, three 'braids' on each side, in which the Roman bride's hair was plaited on her wedding day. A series of verbal adjectives in the sacrifice scene evoke further elements of the Roman marriage ceremony: *sublata uirum*

---

[30] On Ennius' adaptation of Euripides' play, see Jocelyn (1967), 318–42.

[31] Nugent (1994), 205.

[32] Denis Feeney suggests (*per litteras*) that *Aulide* (1.84) alludes to the title of Euripides' tragedy.

[33] Elsom (1992), 217, discussing the scene in which Chaireas watches the (false) death of Callirhoe in Clitophon's *Chaireas and Callirhoe*.

[34] On Iphigenia in Aeschylus and Euripides, see Foley (1985), 68–102; Loraux (1987), 32–48; Marsh (1992); Rabinowitz (1993), 38–54; and Rehm (1994), 50–6.

manibus tremibundaque ad aras | deductast ('lifted aloft in men's hands, she was led trembling to the altar', 1.95–6). The verb *deductast* (1.96) underlines the ominous intersection of sacrifice with marriage here in its evocation of the technical phrase *deductio sponsae in domum mariti*, the escort of the bride from the house of her father to that of her husband; *sublata* (1.95) suggests the Roman custom of lifting the bride over the threshold of the groom's house; and *tremibunda* (1.95) gestures towards the traditional reluctance of the bride on her wedding day. By emphasising Iphigenia's nubile youth, the poet explicitly invites us to recognise the profane coincidence of marriage ritual with sacrificial ritual in the death of Iphigenia:[35] . . . *non ut sollemni more sacrorum | perfecto posset claro comitari Hymenaeo, | sed casta inceste nubendi tempore in ipso | hostia concideret mactatu maesta parentis, | exitus ut classi felix faustusque daretur* ('not that with the solemn custom of rites accomplished she could be accompanied by a ringing wedding-song, but that chaste she might fall in unholy sacrilege at the very season of her marriage, as a sacrificial victim by the slaughter of her father, in order that a fruitful and success- ful departure be granted to the fleet', 1.96–100). Lucretius underscores the Greeks' impious corruption of marriage ritual in the slaughter of Iphigenia by reassigning her generative potential to the Greek fleet through the application of the adjective *felix* ('fruitful, productive, fertile', 1.100) to the departure of the Greeks. The sacrifice of the maiden ensures not the fertility of the bride whose lot is death, but rather the prosperity of the Greek forces whose departure from Aulis brings death to the Trojans, a peculiarly morbid instance of the 'fructifying power of the dead'.[36] Lucretius' account of the sacrifice of Iphigenia thus reveals *in nuce* the complex interrelation of the themes of dirt, disease and death which Nugent identifies as central to the representation of the female elsewhere in *De Rerum Natura*.

Implicit in this nexus is Iphigenia's profound isolation within the

[35] On the conflation of Athenian marital and sacrificial ritual in the portrayal of Iphigenia in Attic drama, see Foley (1982) and Rabinowitz (1993), 31–54; on the confusion of sacrificial ritual with erotic intercourse, see Bataille (1962), 90–3.

[36] Bronfen (1992), 365, employs the phrase in a discussion (364–5) of the Romantic refiguration of the classical muse from the incorporeal divinity of Greek poetry via the corporeally-manifest mistress in Roman elegy (citing Commager (1962), 2–8 and 20–2), into a 'corporally existent beloved' who is now 'dying or already dead' (365) in nineteenth-century literature.

group, an isolation which emerges starkly in Lucretius' handling of the tale. Lucretius emphasises her youth in order to underscore the impiety of her slaughter at the hands of the Greek leaders; and the poet even hints at his own sympathy for her fate in his observation that the onlookers were moved to tears at the sight of her (1.91). Yet looking at Iphigenia is precisely the point of this passage, for only by looking at her sacrifice can we see the injustice of *religio* and therefore respond with an informed Epicurean disavowal of superstition. Iphigenia is isolated before an otherwise all-male group not only by virtue of her sex but also because of her singularity as the object of the sacrificial ritual. Lucretius specifies the participants in the sacrificial ritual as Agamemnon and the male attendants (*et maestum simul ante aras adstare parentem* | *sensit et hunc propter ferrum celare ministros*, 1.89–90) who assist him in his role of sacrificial priest by carrying Iphigenia to the altar (*nam sublata uirum manibus tremibundaque ad aras* | *deductast*, 1.95–6). Moreover, the poet sets the sacrificial scene before an assembly of Greek soldier-citizens who weep at the sight (*aspectuque suo lacrimas effundere ciuis*, 1.91). Iphigenia is thus the object of the combined gaze of the male characters, who stand in here for the poet and his audience.[37] The predominance of male agents in this brief tableau reproduces in small compass the predominance of male characters in the poem and the primacy of men in its implied audience.[38] The poet invites his audience to identify with the male characters who bring about and gaze upon Iphigenia's death, symbolically establishing the hierarchy of gender through the exposure of the dead woman to the public (male) gaze.

The objectifying force of the combined gaze of male poet, readers and characters on the female sacrificial victim undergirds the aestheticisation of her body (parts) in this passage. Lucretius begins with Iphigenia's blood (*sanguine*, 1.85) but dwells on her maidenly locks (*uirgineos comptus*, 1.87), cheeks (*utraque malarum parte*, 1.88) and shaking knees (*genibus summisa*, 1.92), on which the Greek soldiers gaze (*aspectu suo*, 1.91) as she goes trembling (*tremibunda*, 1.95) to her death. By forging an analogy between the display of the bride's liminal sexuality and the display of Iphigenia's death in sacrifice, Lucretius presents Iphigenia as

---

[37] Cf. Marsh (1992), 275–6, on the dynamics of the gaze in the sacrifice of Iphigenia in Aeschylus.

[38] On the predominantly male implied audience of Lucretius' poem, see Nugent (1994).

the object of both an erotic and aesthetic gaze. Although the poet explicitly denies that the spectacle of her death is pleasurable for the onlookers, the accumulation of physical detail in his description of a nubile Iphigenia, whose blood flows in sacrifice rather than in defloration, suggests to the contrary the intersection of Roman male erotic pleasure and violence at the site (and sight) of the beautiful female corpse.[39]

To be sure, Lucretius distances his philosophical project from the superstition central to the myth of the sacrifice of Iphigenia and indeed from the type of literature that traffics in this sort of unedifying tale. He narrates the myth in the high style, using the elevated diction characteristic of and appropriate to heroic epic, notably that of Homer and Ennius who are both named immediately afterwards (1.117–26).[40] Precisely because the myth emblematises the evils of superstition (*tantum religio potuit suadere malorum*, 1.101), Lucretius treats it with all the poetic authority and rhetorical power at his command, with the paradoxical result that the lurid tale of Iphigenia's sacrifice functions as moral exemplum. On the one hand, his procedure implies that the pleasures of heroic epic style and content are congruent, and he suggests that both pleasures will be superseded by the freedom from disturbance promised by Epicurean doctrine. On the other hand, although he discredits the religious superstition that motivates the sacrifice, he nonetheless contrives to rehearse the salacious details of Iphigenia's death. In this way he excites in his audience a delicious pity for the beautiful corpse of the maiden – who is clearly marked as the excluded other. Thus while Lucretius distances himself from the heroic ethic, he is still complicit in the fetishisation of the female corpse for his own project of Epicurean persuasion. In its differential solicitation of male subjects and female object, this passage engages Roman literary, philosophical and cultural technologies of gender in a complicated counterpoint that both undermines and reinforces the Roman sex-gender system.[41]

Unlike Ennius and Lucretius, whose epic narratives engage mythological traditions rich in dead and dying women, Virgil recounts in the *Aeneid* a version of Rome's legendary foundation that was conspicuously

---

[39] On the confusion of eros and sacrifice, cf. Bataille (1962), 90–1, and Fowler (1987), 191–2.

[40] The Homeric name *Iphianassa* (1.85; cf. *Il.* 9.145, 287) is prominent in a passage which contains linguistic features characteristic of Ennian epic.

[41] On Roman sexualities, see Hallett and Skinner (1997).

lacking in them. The hero's wife, conventionally called Eurydice (as in Ennius' account of Ilia's dream), traditionally survived the sack of Troy and accompanied her husband into exile.[42] It was well known that centuries elapsed between the fall of Troy and the *floruit* of Dido, whose love-affair with Aeneas in Virgil's narrative was a scandal in antiquity.[43] The Italian queens Amata and Camilla, moreover, were both shadowy figures.[44] Despite this unpromising material, however, Virgil retains and even enhances the importance of the sacrificial female for the Latin epic plot with the wholesale adaptation of the motif in the *Aeneid*.

Virgil introduces the subject of his poem with a portrait of the hero's divine antagonist, Juno, whose relentless anger (*saeuae memorem Iunonis ob iram*, *Aen.* 1.4), like Achilles' wrath in the *Iliad*, propels the plot of the *Aeneid* from start to finish.[45] Throughout the proem, Virgil metaphorically figures Juno's wrath as a wound, describing her godhead as injured by events at Troy (*numine laeso*, 1.8) and the goddess herself as inflamed in her hostility towards Aeneas by the anger that festers in her heart (1.25–32; cf. *flammato corde*, 1.50). The opening action of the poem proceeds directly from her wound: scarcely have the Trojans set sail from Sicily for Italy when Juno, 'preserving the eternal wound within her breast' (*cum Iuno aeternum seruans sub pectore uulnus*, 1.36), catches sight of them and decides to interfere by stirring up a storm at sea. Since Juno is immortal her wound is metaphorical rather than literal (as Servius recognised), and therefore cannot kill her; but the wounds inflicted on the mortal female characters in the *Aeneid*, and especially on Dido, Juno's avatar, prove lethal.

Already at her earliest appearance in the poem Dido suffers, like her divine patroness, from a 'long injury' (*longa est iniuria*, 1.341).[46] The early application of a metaphorical injury to Dido would be of slight significance were it not for the reappearance of the trope at the opening

---

[42] Heinze (1993), 34 (= (1915), 58); Austin (1964), 286–9; Perkell (1981), 358.

[43] Macr. *Sat.* 5.17.5–6: see further Pease (1935), 14–21 and Horsfall (1973–4).

[44] On Amata see Fordyce (1977), 127, and Lyne (1987), 14–19; on Camilla, see Gransden (1991), 20–5.

[45] On Juno's anger, and its echo of Achilles' wrath, see Levitan (1993), 14–15 and Fowler (1997), 260.

[46] On Virgil's debt to tragic models in his portrait of Dido, see Muecke (1983), with further bibliography; Moles (1984) and (1987); and Hardie (1993), 19–29, and (1997).

of book 4, where Virgil famously characterises Dido as suffering from a burning wound (*at regina graui iamdudum saucia cura | uulnus alit uenis et caeco carpitur igni*, 4.1–2). Dido's metaphorical wound of love receives considerable emphasis in the early part of the book, and Virgil expressly draws the link with Juno by echoing his portrait of the goddess preserving the eternal wound within her breast in a description of the injurious force of Dido's love: *est mollis flamma medullas | interea et tacitum uiuit sub pectore uulnus* ('the soft flame consumes her marrow, and in the meantime the silent wound lives within her breast', 4.66–7). The reminiscence of Juno's injured godhead in the description of Dido's wound links the Carthaginian queen closely to her divine patroness and invites us to see in the fate of Dido a displacement of the motif introduced in connection with Juno. Indeed, Juno's pity for Dido's suffering at the close of the book (4.693–705) may be in some sense motivated by recognition of the displacement of the deadly effect of her own eternal wound on to her protegée.

Virgil follows his elaboration of Dido's metaphorical wound with a simile that implies that her injury will prove fatal:

> uritur infelix Dido totaque uagatur
> urbe furens, qualis coniecta cerua sagitta,
> quam procul incautam nemora inter Cresia fixit
> pastor agens telis liquitque uolatile ferrum
> nescius: illa fuga siluas saltusque peragrat
> Dictaeos; haeret lateri letalis harundo.   (4.68–73)

Unhappy Dido burns, and wanders impassioned in the whole city, just like a deer, struck with an arrow, which all unsuspecting a shepherd shot from afar amid Cretan glades, hunting with his weapons, and unaware he abandoned the flying iron: the deer traverses woods and Cretan pastures in flight; the lethal arrow sticks in her side.

Like the hind of the simile, who is the subject of a verb of motion (*peragrat*, 4.72) and the object of the hunter's active verbs (*fixit*, 4.70; *agens*, 4.71), Dido is the subject of passive and intransitive verbs (*uritur*, *uagatur*, 4.68): both animal and woman are objectified and laid open to our view in the narration. By characterising the arrow that clings in the hind's flank as *letalis*, 'deadly', Virgil intimates that Dido's injury will also lead to her death, and when Dido and Aeneas indulge their passion in the course of a real hunt, the poet explicitly identifies the occasion not only as the source of Dido's ensuing troubles but also as the cause of her death (*ille dies primus leti primusque malorum | causa fuit*, 4.169–70). Thereafter, Virgil repeatedly alludes to the queen's impending death: Dido applies the adjective *moritura*, 'about to die', to herself in her speeches (4.308, 519, 604; *moribunda*, 4.323), and evokes the certainty of her approaching death in her pleas to Aeneas (4.318, 385–7, 436).[47] The poet attributes to Dido a desire for death before her time and thereby exculpates Aeneas from responsibility for it. He thus makes the Carthaginian queen an accomplice to the narrative logic that requires her death.[48]

The second half of the book narrates Dido's elaborate preparations for her death, as Virgil all but ignores his hero to focus the narrative on her 'decision' to die (4.450–1, 474–5, 644). He sets the scene of Dido's death in the innermost part of her palace (*at regina, pyra penetrali in sede sub auras | erecta*, 4.504–5), thereby opening up her dwelling for the viewer's inspection in a way that mirrors on the spatial level the autopsy of her psychological state that he undertakes so effectively in the nine speeches he puts into her mouth in the course of the book.[49] He represents Dido constructing her funeral pyre in such a way that she replicates the marriage-bed she shared with Aeneas (*super exuuias ensemque relictum | effigiemque toro locat*, 4.507–8), so as to confirm the androcentric Roman requirement that she pay for a sexual transgression identified as exclusively hers.

Virgil sends Dido to her death in a lurid tableau far from typical of male death scenes in Latin epic:

> at trepida et coeptis immanibus effera Dido
> sanguineam uoluens aciem, maculisque trementis
> interfusa genas et pallida morte futura,
> interiora domus inrumpit limina et altos
> conscendit furibunda rogos ensemque recludit
> Dardanium, non hos quaesitum munus in usus.

(4.642–7)

---

[47] Cf. the characterisation of Amata as *moritura* (12.55), with Lyne (1987), 116–17.

[48] On the female victim's 'choice', see Kappeler (1986), 148–66; Joplin (1990), 63–4; Bronfen (1992), 269–90; Joshel (1992), 124–8; Rabinowitz (1993), 31–99; and cf. Higonnet (1986).

[49] 4.9–29, 305–30, 365–87, 416–36, 478–98, 534–52, 590–629, 634–40, 651–62.

But fearful and frantic from her huge undertakings, rolling her bloodshot gaze, her trembling cheeks suffused with spots and pale with her death at hand, Dido burst into the inner recesses of the house, climbed the high pyre in a frenzy, and unsheathed the Dardan's sword, a gift not sought for this purpose.

On one level, this description of the queen's wild appearance, especially her bloodshot eyes and the spots on her cheeks, suggests physical illness, an intimation that finds confirmation in Juno's perception of the queen's affliction as a sickness (*quam simul ac tali persensit peste teneri | cara Iouis coniunx*, 4.90–1). Yet Virgil admits an erotic undercurrent into his description of her death with the red-white colour contrast (4.643–4) which conventionally symbolises sexual initiation in Latin poetry and here evokes Dido's sexual transgression in having broken her vow to remain chaste out of piety to her dead husband Sychaeus (4.24–7).[50] The poet emphasises the queen's mad desire for death and conflates this desire with her sexual passion for Aeneas in Dido's action of grasping her lover's sword.

Although Virgil represents Dido taking manifold precautions to safe-guard the secrecy of her purpose and to screen her actions from prying eyes, his depiction of the queen's death exposes her to view: *atque illam media inter talia ferro | conlapsam aspiciunt comites, ensemque cruore | spu-mantem, sparsasque manus* ('and in the midst of such words her compan-ions see her fall on the iron, the sword foaming with blood, her blood-spattered hands', 4.663–5). Dido's companions, unmentioned before, stand in for the hero,[51] as well as the poet and his audience, direct-ing our gaze to the queen's bloody hands and her former lover's dripping sword. Watching Dido die in this fashion confirms not only that the queen must die for her sexual and social transgressions (of Roman norms), but also that she must die so that the man may live.[52] The death of Dido thus emerges as a requirement for Aeneas' foundation of the Roman cultural order. Roman societal norms are proleptically confirmed

---

[50] Cf. Lavinia's blush (12.65–9): on the erotic undertones, see Lyne (1983) and (1987), 114–22; and Fowler (1987) 190–1.

[51] Cf. *Aeneas ... moenia* <u>respiciens</u> *quae iam infelicis Elissae | conlucent flammis* (5.1–4); *Dido ... quam Troius heros | ut primum iuxta stetit* <u>agnouit</u>*que per umbras | obscu-ram, qualem primo qui surgere mense |* <u>aut uidet</u> *aut* <u>uidisse</u> <u>putat</u> *per nubila lunam* (6.450–4).

[52] Catherine Connors suggests (*per litteras*) that Dido must die so that Hannibal may live, since her curse calls for an avenger to arise from her bones (4.625).

and secured over the dead body of a Carthaginian woman whose political activity poses a profound challenge to the nascent Roman order.

Virgil emphasises the narrative necessity of Dido's death and suggests Aeneas' implicit responsibility for it in a final reference to the physical wound gaping in her flesh (*infixum stridit sub pectore uulnus*, 'the wound fixed within her breast hisses', 4.689). The description of her self-injury combines an echo of the metaphorical wound of love which had earlier afflicted her (*tacitum . . . sub pectore uulnus* 4.67) with a reminiscence of the hind simile, the variation of *infixum* for *tacitum* recalling both the shepherd's careless shooting of the deer (*quam . . . fixit | pastor*, 4.70–1) and the lethal force of his arrow (*haeret lateri letalis harundo*, 4.73). Dido's suicide thus literalises Aeneas' rejection of her, and exposes her instrumental function in his epic mission. Aeneas, however, emphatically denies any knowledge of or responsibility for Dido's death in his interview with her in the underworld (6.456–64), and Virgil seems to endorse his hero's view of the matter with his repeated ascription of the language of choice and agency to Dido in book 4.

Philippe Heuzé has demonstrated that there are only two death scenes in the *Aeneid*, those of Dido (4.663–705) and Camilla (11.799–835), in which Virgil prolongs the physical suffering of the characters in artistic development of the spectacle of agony.[53] In both cases, moreover, the poet anticipates the deaths well in advance (4.169–70, 11.587–94). This procedure is especially striking by contrast to Virgil's practice elsewhere in the poem, for he regularly occludes the suffering attendant upon violent death.[54] Heuzé summarises the aesthetic consequences of the depiction of the suffering of Dido and Camilla in an analysis that recalls Poe's observation, cited in the epigraph to my chapter, that the supreme subject of poetry is the death of a beautiful woman:

Virgil perfects a technique of pathos the scope of which is formulated like this: nothing is more moving than death, nothing is

---

[53] Heuzé (1985), 129–34. On Camilla's death, see Fowler (1987), 195–7, with bibliography at 195 n. 38.

[54] Heuzé (1985) identifies two primary techniques for occluding suffering in death scenes: speed (111–28) and aestheticisation (290–5). He notes (292–3) that the suffering of Euryalus (9.435–7) and Pallas (11.68–71) is aestheticised in flower similes drawn from Homer (*Il.* 8.306–8) via Catullus (11.21–4 and 62.39–47): 'in the Latin text what one sees at once is the death-agony of a beautiful flower' (292, my translation).

more touching than a beautiful woman. Consequently, the most compelling subject that an artist could represent is the death of a beautiful woman . . . so Virgil perceives that the body of the woman, more delicate and more moving, reacts better to suffering – or, to put it like painters, that it 'expresses' suffering better, that on it suffering stands out more.[55]

This interpretation of the two women's death-agonies emphasises the aesthetic premium that the (male) poet and his (male) readers realise at the sight of the beautiful female corpse, but fails to account for the gender asymmetry implicit in the paradigm. For the deaths of the two female characters are gratuitous, 'not required by the plot or even the myth',[56] and we might therefore ask what these death-scenes imply about women, death, and the Virgilian epic aesthetic. I suggest that by depicting the death-agonies of Dido and Camilla in such lavish and graphic detail Virgil presents the beautiful woman as the erotic and aesthetic object of his readers' prolonged gaze. He thereby renders the reified female corpse radically distinct not only from the male survivors, the epic hero and his epigones, who gaze upon and profit from her death, but also from the male war dead who perish quickly and apparently without pain in battle.[57]

It is a critical commonplace that both Dido, Aeneas' Carthaginian lover, and Creusa, Aeneas' Trojan wife, are in some sense sacrificed to the hero's mission.[58] In strict chronological sequence, however, Creusa is the first woman sacrificed to the epic plot. It is she who offers the spirited objection to Aeneas' abnegation of his responsibilities to his family that stops the hero from further futile fighting in Troy (2.671–8) and thereby ensures that he witnesses the portent of the flame that encircles Iulus' temples (2.679–86) and finally convinces the reluctant Anchises to leave Troy (2.687–704). Aeneas accordingly leads his household to a shrine of Ceres some distance from the burning city, where he discovers a single desertion from the group: *hic demum collectis omnibus una | defuit; et*

---

[55] Heuzé (1985), 132, my translation.
[56] Rabinowitz (1992), 43, on the suicides of Eurydice (Creon's wife) and Jocasta in Athenian tragedy. Denis Feeney, however, reminds me (*per litteras*) that 'there was a persistent pre-Virgilian version of Dido's death which said that she committed suicide to avoid marriage with a local prince': see Horsfall (1973–4).
[57] Cf. Heuzé (1985), 119.
[58] Perkell (1981); Nugent (1992), 273–8, 287–8. Heuzé (1985), 164–6, and Hardie (1993), 29, discuss Dido's death as self-sacrifice.

comites, natumque, uirumque fefellit ('here at last, one woman alone was missing from the assembled company; she disappointed her comrades, son and husband', 2.743–4).[59]

Creusa's loss constitutes a narrative enigma that engenders her sepulcral reappearance in a passage sketching the central themes of the poem. At the conclusion of the second book, the ghost of Creusa appears to Aeneas and absolves him of responsibility for her loss. Her shade chastises him for opposing the plan of Jove (2.776–9) and prophesies his long wanderings in exile until he reaches Latium and there founds a new kingdom and family with Lavinia (*longa tibi exsilia, et uastum maris aequor arandum;* | *et terram Hesperiam uenies, ubi Lydius arua* | *inter opima uirum leni fluit agmine Thybris.* | *illic res laetae, regnumque, et regia coniunx* | *parta tibi,* 2.780–4). Virgil represents Creusa here freely accepting the necessity of her own death, as she urges Aeneas to do (*lacrimas dilectae pelle Creusae,* 2.784) so that he can realise his epic destiny, for in the very words by which she constitutes herself the first casualty of Aeneas' mission, she imparts his great destiny to her erstwhile husband. If Aeneas seals the success of his imperial mission with the 'sacrifice' of Turnus at the conclusion of the poem (12.950–2),[60] he inaugurates the epic project over the ghostly shade of his wife (2.792–5).

Virgil emblematises the exemplary function of the beautiful female corpse in his epic on the shield of Aeneas, in an ecphrasis that registers the profound distance of Latin from Greek epic and signals Virgil's immense debt to Homer. Modelled on the shield of Achilles in *Iliad* 18, the shield Aeneas carries into battle depicts the history of Rome as a series of military campaigns featuring a succession of Roman heroes. At the centre of the shield Vulcan engraves the battle of Actium and commemorates Augustus' triple triumph after the battle as the culmination of Roman history with the (re)establishment of Roman order (8.675–728). Just as Aeneas inaugurates his imperial mission over his wife's ghost (2.792–5) and reaffirms his devotion to the project over the entreaties of the dying Dido (4.345–50; cf. 6.460–4), so Vulcan depicts Augustus, Aeneas' descendant on the shield, restoring order to the Roman world with the defeat and death of Cleopatra. In the thick of

[59] Perkell (1981), 362, suggests that by phrasing his discovery of Creusa's absence in this way the Virgilian Aeneas implicitly blames his wife for her 'deception'.

[60] Heuzé (1985), 161–4; Hardie (1993), 19–23.

battle, the Egyptian queen is attended by twin snakes (*regina in mediis
. . . | necdum etiam geminos a tergo respicit angues*, 8.696–7), which here
as elsewhere in the poem portend death.[61] Verbal echoes link Cleopatra's
death closely with that of Dido: the Egyptian queen 'grows pale at the
approach of death' (*pallentem morte futura*, 8.709) as the Carthaginian
queen is 'pale with the approach of death' (*pallida morte futura*, 4.644).
Cleopatra's death metonymically represents those of her soldiers, as
Mary Hamer notes: '[t]he visible female body opened and eroticized by
the snakebite guarantee[s] the absent male bodies, opened by weapons, of
the enemies of Rome'.[62] In memorialising the restoration of Roman
order over Cleopatra's corpse, this artefact conjoins the themes of death
and femininity that constitute one paradigm of the Latin epic aesthetic.

Cleopatra is an especially compelling figure for the exploration of
these themes because Octavian's propaganda against Antony and his
Egyptian consort in the years before Actium prompted later historical
commentary on the queen's sexual debauchery and morbid fascination
with death.[63] The fragmentary remains of an early imperial[64] Latin epic
concerning Octavian's campaign against Antony and Cleopatra in Egypt,
the so-called *carmen de bello Actiaco*, reveal the rich literary resonances
of this thematic nexus in connection with the Eyptian queen. Both Virgil
and the anonymous author of the *carmen de bello Actiaco* heavily fore-
shadow Cleopatra's death. Just as Virgil portrays her as shadowed by
snakes already at Actium (*Aen.* 8.696–7) in an allusion to the tradition of
her death by snakebite, so the author of these fragments anticipates her
impending death by stressing the queen's ignorance of her fate: *haec
regina gerit. procul hanc occulta uidebat | Atropos inrid[e]ns [in]ter
diuersa uagantem | consilia interitus, quam iam sua fata manerent* ('the
queen organises these things. From afar Atropos mockingly watched her
wandering amid the various secret plans of death, she whose destiny
already awaited her', col. vii.55–7 Courtney). But the civil war poem's
focus on the events of recent history allows its author to engage in the
sustained characterisation of Cleopatra from which Virgil is precluded in
the *Aeneid* because of his mythological subject matter.

---

[61] Cf. 2.203, 7.450, 8.289.   [62] Hamer (1993), 21.

[63] On her sexual immodesty, see Plu. *Ant.* 26, 53, 58; on her testing of different modes
of death on criminals, see Plu. *Ant.* 71; Ael. *HA* 9.11; Dio Cass. 51.11.2.

[64] The poem's date has been much debated: see Benario (1983) and Courtney (1993),
334, for bibliography and discussion.

The varieties of death which Cleopatra considers are described in lavish detail in two earlier fragments of the poem:

> [dele]ctumqu[e loc]um quo noxia turba co[i]ret
> praeberetque suae spectacula tri[s]tia mortis.
> qualis ad instantis acies cum tela parantur,
> signa, tubae classesque simul terrestribus armis,
> est facies ea uisa loci, cum saeua coirent
> instrumenta necis u[a]rio congesta paratu.
> und[i]que sic illuc campo deforme co[a]ctum
> omne uagabatur leti genus, omne timoris
>
> (col. v.36–43 Courtney)

> aut pendente [su]is ceruicibus aspide mollem
> labitur in somnum trahiturque libidine mortis.
> percutit [ad]flatu breuis hunc sine morsibus anguis
> uolnere seu t[e]nui pars inlita parua ueneni
> ocius interem[i]t, laqueis pars cogitur artis
> in[t]ersaeptam animam pressis effundere uenis,
> i[m]mersisque f[r]eto clauserunt guttura fauces.
> [h]as inter strages solio descendit et inter
>
> (col. vi.45–52 Courtney)

... the chosen place for the crowd of criminals to gather in and offer the sad spectacles of their own death. As when against impending forces weapons are readied, along with standards, military trumpets, and fleets at the same time as land troops, such did the aspect of the place seem, when the savage tools of death, brought together with varied preparation, assembled. Thus gathered there on the field from all sides, every disgusting mode of death wandered, every kind of fear ... or with the asp hanging from his neck, he drifts into soft sleep and is drawn on by desire for death. A small snake kills another by its exhalation, without biting, or a small portion of poison smeared on a slight wound kills more swiftly; some are compelled by tight nooses to expend their blocked breath from compressed passageways; the throats of those immersed in water closed their air-passages. In the midst of this carnage the queen descended from her throne and among ...

The poet represents Cleopatra as both director (cf. *haec regina gerit*, 55) and audience of a spectacular theatre of death, and he even introduces her into the drama she stages when he describes her descent from the throne to mingle with the criminals in their death-agonies (52). She thereby suffers vicariously the deaths of the condemned criminals whom she joins at the moment of their demise. In this way the poet foreshadows her death by snakebite, which he presumably narrated later in the poem. He also admits a sexual undercurrent to the scene in the phrase *libido mortis*, which evokes the commonplace of *amor mortis*.[65] Desire for death is implicit not only in Cleopatra's decision to arrange this display of death-techniques, but also in her participation in the spectacle itself. The author of the *carmen de bello Actiaco* thus both eroticises and aestheticises the morbid tableaux which Cleopatra assembles and enjoys.

The extended description of the queen's theatre of death, coming (as it seems) after a portrait of the victorious Octavian restraining his troops from further killing on the capture of Pelusium (*cum [s]uper[ans La]tius Pelusia [m]oenia Caesar | [coep]erat im[pe]riis animos cohi[be]re su[o]rum*, col. ii.14–15 Courtney), constructs and confirms distinctions between Roman and foreigner, conqueror and conquered, living and dead, male and female. Paradoxically, however, Cleopatra's spectacle seems especially calculated to appeal to a Roman audience since it participates in a distinctly Roman tradition of 'fatal charades'.[66] Long before 29 BCE, when Octavian's henchman Statilius Taurus built the first stone amphitheatre in Rome, the 'murderous games'[67] of gladiatorial combat, wild beast shows, and mass execution of condemned criminals were wildly popular forms of public entertainment at Rome. Staged in the forum until the construction of permanent venues in the imperial period, the Roman games required huge numbers of prisoners of war and condemned criminals, in addition to professional gladiators (themselves usually slaves or condemned criminals), beast-handlers and exotic wild animals.[68] In this context, we may conclude that the spectacular tableaux of death staged by the fictional Cleopatra of the *carmen de bello Actiaco* solicit and satisfy the viewing pleasure of the author's Roman audience.

---

[65] Benario (1983), 1658.
[66] The title of Coleman (1990) about mythological role-playing in the Roman arena; on Roman games, see also Hopkins (1983) and Wiedemann (1992).
[67] The title of Hopkins (1983).   [68] Hopkins (1983), 22–5; Coleman (1990), 54–7.

Such an appeal to Roman tastes and appetites undermines the neat dichotomies outlined above by blurring the divisions between Egypt and Rome. Moreover through a simile that compares Cleopatra's tableaux of death to the spectacle of battle (v.38–41), the poet complicates his own aestheticisation of battle in the poem (coll. i, ii, and viii Courtney). In this way the author of these tantalising fragments both confirms and critiques not only Roman (male) order but also his aesthetic project of memorialising that order over Cleopatra's dead body.

While the poet of the *carmen de bello Actiaco* explores the intersection of death, femininity and the aesthetic on the historical level, Ovid articulates this thematic on the mythological level. In the *Metamorphoses*, the rape and subsequent death of Daphne initiate a series of rapes and gruesome metamorphoses that receive lurid description in the course of the poem.[69] Ovid offers sustained exploration of the intersection of these themes in the narrative of the Trojan war and its aftermath (the return of the Greek warriors and the wanderings of Aeneas), which constitute the supreme subjects of heroic epic (*Met.* 12.4–14.609). His Trojan war narrative opens with a close reworking of Lucretius' treatment of the sacrifice of Iphigenia. Beginning, like Lucretius, with the virgin's blood (*sanguine uirgineo placandam uirginis iram | esse deae*, 12.28–9; cf. *cruorem*, 12.30), Ovid emphasises the prominent role of Agamemnon and his weeping attendants in the ritual (12.30–1), but he disrupts Lucretian expectations by following the version of the story in which a hind is substituted for Iphigenia in the sacrifice (*subposita fertur mutasse Mycenida cerua*, 12.34).[70] The metaphorical association of woman with hind recalls the simile applied to Dido in *Aeneid* 4, and underlines a homology between women and the object of the hunt. Ovid occludes the real physical violence entailed in the sacrifice to titillate his audience by tendering and then withdrawing a display of sacrificial female flesh.[71]

Ovid makes good on the promised display at the conclusion of the war when he narrates the sacrifice of Polyxena (13.439–532), in a passage that also reworks, among several models, Lucretius' narrative of the sacrifice

---

[69] On rape in the *Metamorphoses*, see Richlin (1992a).　　[70] Eur. *I.T.* 28–30.
[71] Cf. Fowler (1989), 96–7, on the narratological and sexual 'tease' implicit in Ovid's placement of the rape of Europa in the book division between *Met.* 2 and 3.

of Iphigenia.[72] Polyxena dies to appease the ghost of Achilles (*placet Achilleos mactata Polyxena manes*, 13.448) in a sacrifice that makes her another bride of death.[73] Ovid implies that Polyxena's sacrifice is analogous to rape (*rapta sinu matris*, 13.450), and he depicts the maiden as uneasily aware not only of the potential for sexual violation inherent in her murder but also of the analogy between the rites of marriage and sacrifice:

> uos modo, ne Stygios adeam non libera manes,
> ite procul, si iusta peto, tactuque uiriles
> uirgineo remouete manus. acceptior illi,
> quisquis is est, quem caede mea placare paratis,
> liber erit sanguis . . .   (13.465–9)

Only you, that I may approach the Stygian shades freely, go away if what I ask is just, and keep your manly hands from touching a maiden. More acceptable to that man, whoever he is whom you prepare to placate with my slaughter, will be free blood.

Polyxena's words conflate the virginity appropriate to a bride with the sacrosanctity of the sacrificial victim, as Ovid represents her taking precautions to veil her person from the sight of the assembled Greek army. She goes to her death intensely aware of herself as an object of the soldiers' collective gaze: *illa super terram defecto poplite labens | pertulit intrepidos ad fata nouissima uultus: | tunc quoque cura fuit partes uelare tegendas, | cum caderet, castique decus seruare pudoris* ('she, falling to the ground with faltering knees, bore an unflinching expression to the end: then too she took care to conceal when she fell the parts which must be covered, and to preserve the glory of her chaste modesty', 13.477–80). Her concern to preserve her modesty even in death implies that the piercing of her body with a sword is analogous to the sexual defloration of the virginal bride. In this context, as Joplin has argued in connection with the

---

[72] *hostia* (Lucr. 1.99, *Met.* 13.452); *sensit* (Lucr. 1.90, *Met.* 13.454); *lacrimas* (Lucr. 1.91, *Met.* 13.474); *concideret* (Lucr. 1.99), *caderet* (*Met.* 13.480); *casta inceste* (Lucr. 1.98), *castique decus seruare pudoris* (*Met.* 13.480). Ovid's specific model for the sacrifice of Polyxena is Cat. 64.362–75; on the use of tragic models in this episode, see Bömer (1982), ad loc.

[73] Cf. Rabinowitz (1993), 244, index s.v. 'marriage-sacrifice link'.

death of Lucretia, 'the "stab to the heart" [cf. *inuitusque sacerdos | prae-bita coniecto rupit praecordia ferro, Met.* 13.475–6], the showable wound, serves as a double for the vagina, the natural opening that must be covered'.[74]

Hecuba's interpretation of her daughter's sacrifice, by contrast, focuses on the violence enacted upon Polyxena's body in the sacrificial ritual. Weeping, she laments her daughter's death and likens it to those of all her sons, killed in war by Achilles (*nata, iaces, uideoque tuum, mea uulnera, uulnus: | en ne perdiderim quemquam sine caede meorum, | tu quoque uulnus habes. at te, quia femina, rebar | a ferro tutam: cecidisti et femina ferro; | totque tuos idem fratres, te perdidit idem, | exitium Troiae nostrique orbator, Achilles*, 13.495–500). Where the Ovidian Polyxena underscores the sexual violation implicit in the act of looking at the female corpse, the Ovidian Hecuba emphasises the physical violence of the sacrifice with her repeated references to Polyxena's 'wound' (13.495, *bis*; 13.497; cf. 13.490), which assimilate her daughter's death in sacrifice to her sons' deaths in battle. Yet by drawing attention to her daughter's wound, Hecuba openly exposes that which Polyxena herself is represented as attempting to conceal. Indeed, the narrative frame of Hecuba's speech underscores this distinction, for we first see Polyxena's wounds when her mother weeps into them (13.490) and her blood when it mats Hecuba's hair (13.492). Ovid thus simultaneously veils and exposes the beautiful female corpse in a sacrifice at once violent and regulatory: over Polyxena's dead body the Greek army seeks to secure a safe return to Greece (13.439–48).

The narrative of Aeneas' wanderings that follows furnishes two variations on the theme. Aeneas and Anchises are hospitably received on the island of Delos by King Anius, who has also seen his family destroyed by the Greek army. Agamemnon demanded the services of his four daughters, whose touch Liber endowed with the ability to transform all matter into food and drink, to provision his army en route to Asia. The king narrates the Greek general's violent seizure of his daughters (*abstrahit inuitas gremio genitoris*, 13.658) in diction that recalls the intimation of sexual violence in Ovid's description of the sacrifice of Polyxena (*rapta sinu matris*, 13.450). Anius' daughters forestall the Greek assault by flight

---

[74] Joplin (1990), 67. Ovid himself employs the motif of falling modestly in his (contemporaneous) account of Lucretia at *F.* 2.833–4.

to their brother Andros in Eubœa, but when the Greek army threatens war he surrenders his sisters. Praying to their patron Liber for aid, they are transformed into birds in a metamorphosis that Anius starkly characterises as slaughter:[75] *tulitque | muneris auctor opem, si miro perdere more | ferre uocatur opem . . . | summa mali nota est: pennas sumpsere tuaeque | coniugis in uolucres, niueas abiere columbas* ('and the author of their gift brought help, if to slay them in an amazing way can be called bringing help . . . the gist of the evil was known: they took on feathers and were transformed into the birds of your wife, snowy doves', 13.669–74). The Greek army's seizure of Anius' daughters initiates a chain of violence that draws into its ambit not only the Greeks, who threaten war in Eubœa even before they reach the Troad, but also Anius' son Andros and the god Liber; death, however, is reserved for Anius' daughters. Ovid thus leaves a succession of dead women – Iphigenia, Anius' daughters, Polyxena – in the train of the Greek expedition to Troy.

At the end of the Trojans' stay on Delos, Aeneas receives as a guest-gift from Anius a cup decorated by the artist Alcon with the deaths of the daughters of Orion. Since the two women's deaths are set in a narrative-ecphrasis relationship to those of Anius' daughters, the poet challenges us to interpret them interactively. On the cup are engraved the seven gates of Thebes and, before the city, tombs and funerary pyres around which women stand in postures of mourning. Ovid here alludes to a plague which once ravaged Thebes and was ended by the sacrifice of Orion's daughters:

> ecce facit mediis natas Orione Thebis,
> hac non femineum iugulo dare uulnus aperto,
> illac demisso per fortia pectora telo
> pro populo cecidisse suo pulchrisque per urbem
> funeribus ferri celebrique in parte cremari.   (13.692–6)

---

[75] The Ovidian Anius problematises the simple equation of metamorphosis with death when he supplements his initial use of *perdere* ('slay', 13.670) with another sense of the verb, *figuram perdere* ('be deprived of their form'): *nec, qua ratione figuram | perdiderint, potui scire, aut nunc dicere possum* ('nor could I recognise by what method they were deprived of their form or even now could I say', 13.671–2). The kaleidoscopic sequence of death (Polyxena), substitution of a lower animal (Iphigenia), and metamorphosis into a lower animal (Anius' daughters), exemplifies the metamorphic variety of Ovid's Trojan war narrative and constitutes a sophisticated commentary on the meaning of metamorphosis itself.

Look, in the middle of Thebes he engraves the daughters of Orion:
on this side they offer unwomanly wounds to their bared throats, on
that, the weapon plunged into their valiant breasts, they lie dead on
behalf of the people and, carried through the city in beautiful
funerary procession, are cremated in the thronging square.

A conventional analogy between war and pestilence (cf. *Il.* 1.9–100)
underpins the passage and links it thematically to the sacrifices of
Iphigenia, Polyxena and the daughters of Anius in this section of the
Metamorphoses.[76] Just as the sacrifices of Iphigenia and Polyxena benefit
the Greek military community of survivors, so the sacrifice of Orion's
daughters benefits the Theban community, in another instance of 'the
fructifying power of the dead' that recalls the deaths of Ilia, Iphigenia
and Creusa in earlier Latin epic. Paradoxically, this sacrifice even ensures
the continuity of the male line, for from the ashes of Orion's daughters
arise twin youths, the Coronae, who lead the funeral procession in
honour of their 'mothers' (*tum de uirginea geminos exire fauilla,* | *ne genus
intereat, iuuenes, quos fama Coronas* | *nominat, et cineri materno ducere
pompam, Met.* 13.697–9). The ecphrasis exposes the thematic centrality
of the beautiful female corpse to the aesthetic project of Latin epic.
Memorialised on Alcon's cup, Orion's daughters die quite literally for the
viewing pleasure of the epic hero Aeneas and his readers.

The ecphrastic articulation of this thematic nexus, already discussed in
connection with the shield of Aeneas in the *Aeneid*, continues in Flavian
epic. In the *Punica*, an ecphrasis early in the poem illustrates the structural relations that found the master plot of Silian epic on the spectacle of
female death. Before the battle of Saguntum, the Ocean tribes of Spain
present Hannibal with a set of armour that includes a breast-plate of
bronze and iron overlaid with gold on which Gallician craftsmen have
wrought designs (*Pun.* 2.395–405). The first scene Hannibal surveys on
this cuirass depicts Dido's foundation of Carthage. Silius briefly summarises the contents of *Aeneid* 4 to recall Dido's building programme, her
welcome of the ship-wrecked Trojans, the lovers' secret tryst in the cave
when the storm scatters the hunt, and Aeneas' departure (2.406–25). By
reproducing the 'highlights' of the Virgilian narrative, the Flavian poet

[76] Dowden (1989), 168, analyses the structural connections linking the tale (as attested
in Nicander, *apud* Ant. Lib. *Met.* 25) with other myths of maiden sacrifice.

retains Virgil's emphasis on the wounded queen's stage-managed death (*ipsa, pyram super ingentem stans, saucia Dido | mandabat Tyriis ultricia bella futuris, Pun.* 2.422–3) and the spectacle her agony furnishes to the Roman epic hero and his readers (*ardentemque rogum media spectabat ab unda | Dardanus et magnis pandebat carbasa fatis*, 2.424–5). Aeneas' great destiny is here clearly achieved at the cost of Dido's life, yet Hannibal proudly outfits himself in the armour, mistakenly believing it to betoken success against the Romans (2.453–6). Dido's death functions in the *Punica* both to confirm Roman power for Silius' Roman readership and to initiate the conflict with Carthage that constitutes the subject of Silius' song.

The spectacle of Dido's death on Hannibal's shield pointedly recalls the opening scene of the epic, which Silius sets in a temple precinct at the centre of Carthage. Constructed on the very site of Dido's death (*hoc sese, ut perhibent, curis mortalibus olim | exuerat regina loco*, 1.85–6), the temple is sacred to the dead queen (*sacrum genetricis Elissae | manibus*, 1.81–2) and houses a marble statue of her, flanked by those of Sychaeus and her ancestors, with Aeneas' sword at her feet. Her effigy presides over the chthonic rites performed by her priestess (1.93–6), and even symbolically participates in those rites (*tum magico uolitant cantu per inania manes | exciti, uultusque in marmore sudat Elissae*, 1.97–8). Here Hannibal swears by Dido's ghost to undertake war with the Romans when he comes of age (1.99–119): *hanc mentem iuro nostri per numina Martis, | per manes, regina, tuos* ('I swear this purpose by the power of our war-god and by your shade, queen', 1.118–19). The dead queen's body grounds the very architecture of the poem, thereby lending her uncanny authority to Silius' narrative.

Elsewhere in early imperial Latin epic too, dead and dying women initiate the action of the narrative. Lucan, for example, founds civil war – subject and title of his poem – in part on Julia's death (*morte tua discussa fides bellumque mouere | permissum ducibus*, 1.119–20), and at the opening of book three her ghost appears in a nightmare-vision to her former husband to goad him into the conflict with her father (3.1–45). Statius gestures towards the genre's aesthetic investment in the beautiful female corpse at the outset of the *Thebaid*, where he ponders opening the poem with the rape of Europa or the deaths of Amphion's wives (1.3–14). At the end of classical antiquity, Claudian explores the thematic conjunction of death, femininity and the aesthetic in his unfinished *De Raptu Proserpinae*. Taking the rape of Proserpina by Pluto, king of the underworld (1.26–8), as his subject, Claudian elaborates the intersection of marriage and death in the rape as the central theme of his most ambitious poem.

The theme is also implicit in Valerius' handling of the myth of Phrixus and Helle in the *Argonautica*. The Valerian Pelias invokes the shades of Helle and Phrixus when he commissions Jason to recover the golden fleece (1.41–50), the goal of the Argonauts' expedition to which Jason refers initially as 'the fleece of Helle' (1.167; cf. 1.425).[77] Claiming that his sleep is troubled by the unquiet ghosts of Phrixus and Helle, Pelias demands that Jason avenge their deaths. His invocation of Phrixus is elsewhere shown to be a self-serving lie, however, for Phrixus not only survives his journey to Colchis on the back of the ram, but is cordially received into both the country and the family of Aeetes, who marries one of his daughters to the Greek stranger (1.520–4). The death of Helle thus emerges as the sole legitimate motivation for the Argonauts' voyage of reparation, and so Orpheus presents it. He recounts her tragic death the evening before the Argonauts depart in a song that adheres closely to the familiar thematic paradigm, as befits the exemplary epic song of the exemplary epic singer (1.277–93).

Orpheus' song locates the origins of the Argonauts' expedition in Helle's pathetic death at sea and challenges the first Greek sailors to succeed where she so lamentably failed, in a concentrated statement of the poem's central theme. Fully half of Orpheus' song is devoted to the elaboration of Helle's death at sea (1.286–93). First picturing her sitting astride the ram (1.282), the bard emphasises the pathos (cf. *heu*, 1.287) inherent in Helle's 'desertion' of her brother (*hic soror Aeoliden ... deserit*, 1.286–7) and her desperate attempts to cling to the ram's fleece (1.288–9) until she finally sinks beneath the waves, drawn down by the weight of her wet garments (1.289–90). Stricken with grief, her brother watches her die, apparently unable to save her though she beseeches him for aid: *quis tibi, Phrixe, dolor, rapido cum concitus aestu | respiceres miserae clamantia uirginis ora | extremasque manus sparsosque per aequora crines!* ('what was your grief Phrixus, when you, spurred on by the swift

---

[77] More frequently, however, Valerius describes it as 'the fleece of Phrixus' (1.272–3, 328, 377; 4.556; 5.632; 6.11, 150, 593; 7.14; 8.267–8).

swell, looked back upon the piteous maiden's face as she cried out, the tips of her hands, and her hair spread out over the surf,' 1.291–3). Unlike Phrixus, whose gaze focalises Orpheus' song for the Argonauts (and Valerius' readers), Helle is anatomised as she succumbs to her fate – palms, face, hands and hair scattered over the sea.

Orpheus' focus on Helle emerges particularly clearly from comparison with the cosmogonic song of Apollonius' Orpheus, who makes no mention of Helle although he sings at the corresponding point of the Greek poet's *Argonautika* (1.496–511). Indeed she is almost completely absent from Apollonius' poem, receiving only one explicit reference (1.256) and an etymologising allusion (1.927). In Valerius' poem, by contrast, Helle herself even appears before the Argonauts in an epiphany to offer them guidance in the form of a prophecy (2.587–612). Addressing Jason, she likens the Argonauts' undertaking to her own ill-fated journey across the sea: *te quoque ab Haemoniis ignota per aequora terris | regna infesta domus fatisque simillima nostris | fata ferunt; iterum Aeolios Fortuna penates | spargit et infelix Scythicum gens quaeritis amnem* ('a hostile kingdom at home and a destiny similar to my own carries you too away from Thessaly over unknown seas; again Chance scatters Aeolus' household gods and you, unhappy people, seek the Scythian stream', 2.592–5). In a speech designed primarily to strengthen the Argonauts' resolve and to foreshadow their ultimate success (2.596–7), she advises them to secure Phrixus' goodwill by paying due rites at his burial mound before proceeding to Colchis (2.598–600), and asks them to remember her to her brother's shade:

> '. . . cinerique, precor, mea reddite dicta:
> non ego per Stygiae quod rere silentia ripae,
> frater, agor; frustra uacui scrutaris Aurni,
> care, uias. neque enim scopulis me et fluctibus actam
> frangit hiemps; celeri extemplo subiere ruentem
> Cymothoe Glaucusque manu; pater ipse profundi
> has etiam sedes, haec numine tradidit aequo
> regna nec Inois noster sinus inuidet undis.'   (2.600–7)

'. . . and to his ashes, I pray you, return my words: I am not driven, as you think brother, through the silent haunts of the Stygian shore; in vain, my dear, do you search the roads of empty Avernus. For no storm breaks me driven on rocks and waves; Cymothoe and Glaucus

helped me at once with a swift hand as I fell; the father of the deep
himself allotted me this abode even and this kingdom, with just
purpose, nor does our gulf envy Ino's waves.'

Helle here, like Creusa in *Aeneid* 2, is represented as acquiescing in the
justice (*numine . . . aequo*, 2.606) of her fate. Yet despite her accession to
divinity among the sea-gods, Valerius implies that she still grieves this
'death' at sea, for her demeanour as she sinks once more beneath the
waves remains sad (*maestos tranquilla sub aequora uultus | cum gemitu
tulit*, 2.608–9).

The death of a beautiful woman repeatedly serves as the catalyst in
Latin epic for the epic hero's assertion of political agency. Violence in
Latin epic is unleashed first upon the eroticised female body, and this
initial violence 'displaces responsibility for what follows onto the
victim'.[78] The death of an 'innocent' woman – Ilia, Iphigenia, Creusa,
Polyxena, the daughters of Anius and Orion, Helle – legitimates the epic
hero's violent mission: over her dead body, he regenerates or transforms
the social order. Similarly, the death of a 'dangerous' woman – Dido,
Cleopatra, Camilla – authorises the epic hero's establishment of a normative order imperilled by her deviance.[79] The result is the same whether
the political order is implicitly critiqued (as it is in the death of an innocent woman) or confirmed (as it is in the death of a dangerous woman):
the female corpse guarantees the stability of the cultural order achieved
in the poem. Roman epic poetry thus produces the social order and the
male political subject 'at the expense of and through the construction of
the female as object'.[80] By guaranteeing the stability of the male political
order, the dead woman offers further confirmation of the social structure
of gender that subtends Roman culture. The female corpse in these
poems is both the site of male mastery and the locus of a rhetoric of violence that repeats and reinforces the occlusion and elision of women's
agency in the larger culture.

The Latin epic tradition nonetheless offers a forum in which to articulate a critique of this paradigm, as we saw in Lucretius' portrait of
Iphigenia, where the spectacle of female death provokes an explicit cri-

---

[78] Cf. Joplin (1990), 59–68, discussing Livy's Lucretia, quote at 60.
[79] On the functional interchangeability of the death of innocent and deviant women,
see Bronfen (1992), 181.
[80] Rabinowitz (1992), 51, on the structure of identification in Athenian tragedy.

tique of the heroic ethos central to the genre. And indeed the very fre-
quency with which the rhetorical gestures of occlusion and elision occur,
both in the Latin epic tradition and in individual instances of it (especially in the *Aeneid* and the *Metamorphoses*), complicates the sense in
which the poems successfully occlude or elide female subjectivity. For
how effective a denial of female agency is really on offer, in a literary tradition that repeatedly represents the aspirations of female characters to
participate in the heroic (male) world and consistently contains those
aspirations? If no Latin epic is complete without the death agony of a
woman, no gesture of such occlusion finally succeeds. In addition, the
centrality of female death in the Latin epic narrative (a book and a half
for Dido, a third of a book each for Camilla and Asbyte, as well as an
entire poem on Proserpina's marriage to death and, perhaps, an entire
poem for Cleopatra) works to undermine the genre's denial of female
subjectivity. Beyond Latin epic, Dido herself is treated with explicit sympathy not only in *Heroides* 7 (which participates in an elegiac tradition of
inverting the epic world-view),[81] but also in late antique examples of phil-
ological commentary and Christian theology.[82] This literature alerts us to
the imaginative energy mobilised but not finally expended in the Latin
epic tradition with the representation of female characters, and suggests
that the division between confirming and critiquing a masculine world
order remains open to debate.

[81] Desmond (1993), and Wyke (1995), 124.
[82] Macr. *Sat.* 5.17.5–6; Serv. on *Aen.* 4.36; Tert. *ad nat.* 1.18, 2.9, *apol.* 50, *ad martyr.*
4; Min. Fel. 20.6; Jer. *adu. Iouin.* 1.43; Aug. *Conf.* 1.13.21. See further Pease (1935),
64–7.

Epilogue

When I told a graduate mentor that I was developing a course on women in epic he responded: 'You don't teach women in epic; you teach women in tragedy. There are no women in epic.' My aim in this study has been precisely to restore female characters to visibility in Latin epic and to examine the discursive operations that effect their marginalisation within the genre and the critical tradition it has engendered. As the most widely disseminated form of poetry performed by and for an elite Roman male audience, Latin epic constituted an important social technology for the construction and negotiation of gender difference in ancient Rome. The asymmetrical gender relations on display in the genre both reflect, and reflect upon, Roman hierarchies of gender.

Roman epicists repeatedly give voice to female characters and thereby open up for scrutiny the masculine worldview the genre characteristically proposes, even if individual instantiations of epic frequently work to foreclose the production of meanings that may undermine male structures of authority. Stephen Hinds has recently suggested that while women's entry into heroic narrative disturbs the discursive field of Latin epic, the expression of surprise at their presence comes to constitute a normative feature of the genre.[1] The preceding chapters lend support to this paradoxical formulation, for if they have argued that the female is employed by epic texts (and their critics) primarily with reference to the male, they have also documented the genre's pervasive association of women with the 'public' sphere, in their cultural and metaphorical relations to Roman imperialism, militarism and colonisation. Many themes

[1] Hinds (n.d.).

132

invite further treatment, especially in connection with the 'private' sphere:[2] the genre's uneasy recognition that male glory may be memorialised not only in epic verse but also in female lamentation;[3] the role of bearing and rearing the male children who will grow up to be heroes; women's textile production and its relation to the Roman epicists' production of text; and the question of inset female narrative within Latin epic. The genre's negotiation of modes of masculinity also requires further scrutiny.[4]

A final area of investigation that my study has not attempted will be difficult given the state of our evidence: an examination of non-institutional, non-elite, and non-male responses to the representation of women in Latin epic. On the evidence of Juvenal's *Satires* we might assume that women responded to the *Aeneid* most passionately by identifying with Dido (*illa tamen grauior, quae cum discumbere coepit | laudat Vergilium, periturae ignoscit Elissae, | committit uates et comparat, inde Maronem | atque alia parte in trutina suspendit Homerum*, 'but that woman is worse who, when she sits down to dinner, praises Virgil, makes allowances for Elissa on her deathbed, and matches the poets for comparison, setting Virgil in one side of the balance, Homer in the other', 6.434–7), but only careful examination of the reception history of epic at Rome will enable us to map the full dynamics of the reproduction and interrogation of Roman economies of gender in Latin epic. This study will have achieved its aims if it has contributed to the current scrutiny of gender and genre in Latin literature and Roman culture by investigating how the genre of epic represents gender difference and solicits gender identification.

---

[2] A start in Wiltshire (1989) and Nugent (1992).
[3] The Greek material has been discussed by Holst-Warhaft (1992).
[4] Exemplary studies are Fowler (1987), Hardie (1993), and Oliensis (1997).

Bibliography

Adams, J.N. (1982) *The Latin sexual vocabulary*. Baltimore

Ahl, F.M. (1976) *Lucan, an introduction*. Ithaca and London

(1984) 'The rider and the horse: politics and power in Roman poetry from Horace to Statius', *ANRW* II.32.1: 40–110

(1986) 'Statius' "Thebaid": a reconsideration', *ANRW* II.32.5: 2803–912

Althusser, L. (1971) *Lenin and philosophy*. New York

Ardener, E. (1975) 'Belief and the problem of women', in S. Ardener (ed.), *Perceiving women*, 1–27. London and New York

Aricò, G. (1991) 'La vicenda di Lemno in Stazio e Valerio Flacco', in Korn and Tschiedel (1991), 197–210

Arthur, M.B. (1981) 'The divided world of *Iliad* VI', in Foley (1981), 19–44

Arthur Katz, M.B. (1992) *Penelope's renown*. Ithaca

Austin, R.G. (1964) (ed.) *P. Vergili Maronis Aeneidos liber secundus*. Oxford

Bailey, C. (1947) (ed.) *Titi Lucreti Cari, De Rerum Natura libri sex*, with prolegomena, critical apparatus, translation and commentary, 3 vols. Oxford

Bakhtin, M.M. (1981) 'Epic and novel', trans. C. Emerson and M. Holquist, in M. Holquist (ed.), *The dialogic imagination*, 3–40. Austin

Bataille, G. (1962) *Erotism: death and sensuality*, trans. M. Dalwood. New York

Beard, M. (1989) 'Acca Larentia gains a son: myths and priesthood at Rome', in M.M. Mackenzie and C. Roueché (eds.), *Images of authority: papers presented to Joyce Reynolds on the occasion of her 70th birthday*, 41–61. Cambridge

(1995) 'Re-reading vestal virginity', in R. Hawley and B. Levick (eds.), *Women in antiquity: new assessments*, 166–77. London and New York

Benario, H.W. (1983) 'The "carmen de bello Actiaco" and early imperial epic', *ANRW* II.30.3: 1656–62

Bergren, A. (1980) 'Helen's web: time and tableau in the *Iliad*', *Helios* 7: 19–34

(1981) 'Helen's "good drug": *Odyssey* IV 1–305', in S. Kresic (ed.), *Contemporary literary hermeneutics and interpretation of classical texts*, 201–14. Ottawa

Bloch, A. (1970) '*Arma uirumque* als heroische Leitmotiv', *MH* 27: 206–11

Bolgar, R.R. (1954) *The classical heritage and its beneficiaries*. Cambridge

Bömer, F. (1969–86) *P. Ovidius Naso, Metamorphosen: Kommentar*, 7 vols. Heidelberg

Bonner, S.F. (1977) *Education in ancient Rome*. Berkeley

Bourdieu, P. (1977) *Outline of a theory of practice*, trans. R. Nice. Cambridge

(1984) *Distinction: a social critique of the judgement of taste*, trans. R. Nice. Cambridge, MA

(1990) *The logic of practice*, trans. R. Nice. Cambridge

Bourdieu, P. and Passeron, J.-C. (1977) *Reproduction in education, society and culture*, trans. R. Nice. London and Beverly Hills

Bourdieu, P. *et al.* (1994) *Academic discourse*, trans. R. Teese. Stanford

Boyle, A.J. (1988) (ed.) *The imperial muse: to Juvenal through Ovid*. Victoria, Australia

(1990) (ed.) *The imperial muse: Flavian epicist to Claudian*. Victoria, Australia

(1993) (ed.) *Roman epic*. London

(1995 (ed.) *Roman literature and ideology. Ramus essays for J.P. Sullivan*. Victoria, Australia

Brehaut, E. (1912) *An encyclopedist of the dark ages: Isidore of Seville*. New York

Bremmer, J.N. and Horsfall, N.M. (1987). *Roman myth and mythography*. London

Bronfen, E. (1992) *Over her dead body: death, femininity and the aesthetic*. New York

Brunt, P.A. (1978) '*Laus Imperii*', in P.D.A. Garnsey and C.R. Whittaker (eds.), *Imperialism in the ancient world*, 159–91. Cambridge

Büchner, K. (1982) *Fragmenta poetarum Latinorum*. Stuttgart

Burkert, W. (1979) *Structure and history in Greek mythology and ritual*. Berkeley, Los Angeles, and London

(1983) *Homo necans: the anthropology of ancient Greek sacrificial ritual and myth*, trans. P. Bing. Berkeley, Los Angeles, and London

Butler, J. (1990) *Gender trouble*. New York and London

Caplan, P. (1987) *The cultural construction of sexuality*. London

Cheyfitz, E. (1997) *The poetics of imperialism*. Philadelphia

Clay, D. (1983) *Lucretius and Epicurus*. Ithaca and London

Coleman, K.M. (1990) 'Fatal charades: Roman executions staged as mythological enactments', *JRS* 80: 44–73

Collier, J.F., and Rosaldo, M.Z. (1981) 'Politics and gender in simple societies', in Ortner and Whitehead (1981), 275–329

Collins, L. (1988) *Studies in characterization in the Iliad*. Frankfurt am Main

Commager, S. (1962) *The Odes of Horace*. New Haven

Connors, C.M. (1994) 'Ennius, Ovid and representations of Ilia', *MD* 32: 99–112

Conte, G.B. (1986) *The rhetoric of imitation*, ed. C. Segal. Ithaca [Originally published in Italian in two volumes, *Memoria dei poeti e sistema letterario: Catullo, Virgilio, Ovidio, Lucano*. Turin, 1974; and *Il genere e i suoi confini: Cinque studi sulla poesia di Virgilio*. Turin, 1984]

(1994) *Latin literature: a history*, trans. J.B. Solodow; rev. D. Fowler and G.W. Most. Baltimore [Originally published in Italian as *Letteratura latina: Manuale storico dalle origini alla fine dell' impero romano*. Florence, 1987]

Cooper, H.M., Munich, A.A., and Squier, S.M. (eds.) (1989) *Arms and the woman: war, gender, and literary representation*. Chapel Hill

(1989a) 'Arms and the woman: the con[tra]ception of the war text', in Cooper, Munich, Squier (1989), 9–24

Corbier, M. (1995) 'Male power and legitimacy through women: the *domus Augusta* under the Julio-Claudians', in R. Hawley and B. Levick (eds.), *Women in antiquity: new assessments*, 178–93. London and New York

Courtney, E. (1993) *Fragmentary Latin poets*. Oxford

Curtius, E.R. (1953) *European literature and the Latin middle ages*. Princeton

D'Ambra, E. (1993) *Private lives, imperial virtues*. Princeton

de Jong, I.J.F. (1987) *Narrators and focalizers*. Amsterdam

De Lauretis, T. (1984) *Alice doesn't*. Bloomington

(1986) (ed.) *Feminist studies / critical studies*. Bloomington

(1987) *Technologies of gender*. Bloomington

Delia, D. (1991) 'Fulvia reconsidered', in S.B. Pomeroy (ed.), *Women's history and ancient history*, 197–217. Chapel Hill and London

Desmond, M. (1993) 'When Dido reads Virgil: gender and intertextuality in Ovid's *Heroides* 7', *Helios* 20, 56–68

(1994) *Reading Dido: gender, textuality, and the medieval 'Aeneid'*. Minneapolis and London

Dewar, M. (1991) (ed.) *Statius, Thebaid IX*. Oxford

Doherty, L. (1995) *Siren songs*. Ann Arbor

Dominik, W.J. (1990) 'Monarchal power and imperial politics in Statius' *Thebaid*', in Boyle (1990), 74–97

(1993) 'From Greece to Rome: Ennius' *Annales*', in Boyle (1993), 37–58

(1994) *The mythic voice of Statius: power and politics in the Thebaid*. Leiden

Donaldson, I. (1982) *The rapes of Lucretia: a myth and its transformations*. Oxford

Dougherty, C. (1993) *The poetics of colonization*. Oxford

Douglas, M. (1966) *Purity and danger*. London

Dowden, K. (1989) *Death and the maiden: girls' initiation rites in Greek mythology*. London and New York

DuBois, P. (1982) *Centaurs and Amazons*. Ann Arbor

(1988) *Sowing the body*. Chicago

Edwards, C. (1993) *The politics of immorality*. Cambridge

Elshtain, J.B. (1987) *Women and war*. London

Elsom, H.E. (1992) 'Callirhoe: displaying the phallic woman', in Richlin 1992, 212–30

Endt, J. (1969) (ed.) *Adnotationes super Lucanum*. Stuttgart

Feeney, D.C. (1991) *The gods in epic*. Oxford

Felson-Rubin, N. (1994) *Regarding Penelope: from courtship to poetics*. Princeton

Finley, M.I. (1978) 'Empire in the Greco-Roman world', *G&R* 25: 1–15

Flory, M.B. (1993) 'Livia and the history of public honorific statues for women in Rome', *TAPhA* 123: 287–308

Foley, H.P. (1978) '"Reverse similes" and sex roles in the *Odyssey*', *Arethusa* 11: 7–26

(1981) (ed.) *Reflections of women in antiquity*. New York

(1982) 'Marriage and sacrifice in Euripides' *Iphigeneia in Aulis*', *Arethusa* 15: 159–80

(1985) *Ritual irony: poetry and sacrifice in Euripides*. Ithaca and London

Fordyce, C.J. (1977) *P. Vergili Maronis Aeneidos libri VII – VIII, with a commentary*. Oxford

Fowler, D.P. (1987) 'Vergil on killing virgins', in Whitby, Hardie, Whitby (1987), 185–98
  (1989) 'First thoughts on closure: problems and prospects', *MD* 22: 75–122
  (1997) 'Virgilian narrative: story-telling', in Martindale (1997), 259–70
Fraenkel, E. (1990) 'Aspects of the structure of *Aeneid* 7', in Harrison (1990), 253–76; reprinted from *JRS* 35 (1945): 1–14
Fraschetti, A. (1984) 'La sepoltura delle Vestali e la città', in *Du châtiment dans la cité: supplices corporels et peine de mort dans le monde antique*. Table ronde organisée par l'École française de Rome avec le concours du Centre national de la recherche scientifique (Rome 9–11 novembre 1982), 97–129. Paris and Rome
Fredricksmeyer, E.A. (1985) 'Structural perspectives in *Aeneid* VII', *CJ* 80: 228–37
Gale, M.R. (1994) *Myth and poetry in Lucretius*. Cambridge
Galinsky, K. (1996) *Augustan culture*. Princeton
Gardner, J.F. (1995) 'Gender-role assumptions in Roman law', *EMC/CV* n.s. 14: 377–400
Gentilcore, R. (1995) 'The landscape of desire: the tale of Pomona and Vertumnus in Ovid's *Metamorphoses*', *Phoenix* 49: 110–20
Georgii, H. (1905–6) (ed.) *Tiberi Claudi Donati interpretationes Vergilianae*, 2 vols. Leipzig
Gleason, M. (1995) *Making men*. Princeton
Goldberg, S.M. (1995) *Epic in republican Rome*. Oxford
Götting, M. (1969) *Hypsipyle in der Thebais des Statius*. Wiesbaden
Gransden, K.W. (1991) (ed.) *Virgil, Aeneid book XI*. Cambridge
Griffin, J. (1980) *Homer on life and death*. Oxford
Guillory, J. (1993) *Cultural capital*. Chicago and London
Habinek, T.N. (1988) 'Greeks and Romans in book 12 of Quintilian', in Boyle (1988), 192–202
Hainsworth, J.B. (1991) *The idea of epic*. Berkeley, Los Angeles, and London
Hallett, J.P. (1977) '*Perusinae glandes* and the changing image of Augustus', *AJAH* 2: 151–71
Hallett, J.P. and Skinner, M.B. (1997) (eds.) *Roman sexualities*. Princeton
Hamer, M. (1993) *Signs of Cleopatra*. London
Hardie, P. (1986) *Virgil's Aeneid: cosmos and imperium*. Oxford
  (1990) 'Ovid's Theban history: the first "anti-*Aeneid*"?' *CQ* 40: 224–35
  (1990a) 'Flavian epicists on Virgil's epic technique', in Boyle (1990), 3–20
  (1993) *The epic successors of Virgil*. Cambridge
  (1994) (ed.) *Virgil, Aeneid IX*. Cambridge
  (1997) 'Virgil and tragedy', in Martindale (1997), 312–26
Harris, W.R. (1979) *War and imperialism in republican Rome, 327–70 BC*. Oxford
  (1989) *Ancient literacy*. Cambridge, MA
Harrison, S.J. (ed.) (1990) *Oxford readings in Vergil's Aeneid*. Oxford
  (1991) *Vergil, Aeneid 10*. Oxford
Havelock, E. (1963) *Preface to Plato*. Oxford
Heinze, R. (1993) *Virgil's epic technique*, trans. H. Harvey, D. Harvey and F. Robertson. Bristol [Originally published in German as *Virgils epische Technik*. Berlin, 1915]

Helms, L. (1989) '"Still wars and lechery": Shakespeare and the last Trojan woman', in Cooper, Munich and Squier (1989), 25–42

Hemker, J. (1985) 'Rape and the founding of Rome', *Helios* 12: 41–47

Henderson, Jeffrey. (1991) *The maculate muse.*[2] New York and Oxford

Henderson, John. (1987) 'Suck it and see', in Whitby, Hardie, Whitby (1987), 105–18

(1988) 'Lucan/the word at war', in Boyle (1988), 122–64

(1989) 'Satire writes "woman": *gendersong*', *PCPhS* 215: 50–80

(1991) 'Statius' *Thebaid*/form premade', *PCPhS* 37: 30–80

(1993) 'Form remade/Statius' *Thebaid*', in Boyle (1993), 162–191

(1994) '*Danaos timeo*: Amazons in Greek art and poetry', in S. Goldhill and R. Osborne (eds.), *Art and text in ancient Greek culture*, 85–137. Cambridge

Heuzé, P. (1985) *L'image du corps dans l'œuvre de Virgile.* Paris and Rome

Higgins, L.A. and Silver, B.R. (1991) (eds.) *Rape and representation.* New York

Higonnet, M.R. (1986) 'Speaking silences: women's suicide', in Suleiman (1986), 68–83

(1989) 'Civil wars and sexual territories', in Cooper, Munich and Squier (1989), 80–96

Hill, D.E. (1990) 'Statius' *Thebaid*: a glimmer of light in a sea of darkness', in Boyle (1990), 98–118

Hillard, T. (1989) 'Republican politics, women, and the evidence', *Helios* 16: 165–82

Hinds, S.E. (1998) *Allusion and intertext: dynamics of appropriation in Roman poetry.* Cambridge

(n.d.) 'Essential epic: genre and gender from Macer to Statius', paper delivered at the Center for Hellenic Studies Colloquium 'Matrices of genre: authors, canons and society', Washington 1996

Hollis, A.S. (1996) 'Traces of ancient commentaries on Ovid's *Metamorphoses*', *PLLS* 9: 159–74

Holmberg, I. (1995) 'The *Odyssey* and female subjectivity', *Helios* 22: 103–22

Holst-Warhaft, G. (1992) *Dangerous voices.* London and New York

Homans, M. (1987) 'Feminist criticism and theory: the ghost of Creusa', *Yale Journal of Criticism* 1.1: 153–82

Hopkins, K. (1983) 'Murderous games' in K. Hopkins, *Death and renewal: sociological studies in Roman history* 2, 1–30. Cambridge

Horsfall, N.M. (1971) 'Numanus Remulus: ethnography and propaganda in *Aeneid* 9.598ff.', *Latomus* 30, 1108–16; reprinted in Harrison (1990), 305–15

(1973–4), 'Dido in the light of history', *PVS* 13: 1–13; reprinted in Harrison (1990), 127–44

(1987) '*Non viribus aequis*: some problems in Virgil's battle-scenes', *G&R* 34: 48–55

(1989) 'Aeneas the colonist', *Vergilius* 35: 8–27

Hübner, W. (1970) *Dirae in römischen Epos: über das Verhältnis von Vogeldämonen und Prodigien.* Hildesheim

Hunter, R. (1993) *The 'Argonautica' of Apollonius.* Cambridge

Huston, N. (1986) 'The matrix of war: mothers and heroes', in Suleiman (1986), 119–38

Jahnke, R. (1898) (ed.) *Lactantii Placidi qui dicitur commentarii in Statii Thebaida et commentarius in Achilleida.* Leipzig

Jocelyn, H.D. (1967) (ed.) *The tragedies of Ennius.* Cambridge

Jones, B.W. (1992) *The emperor Domitian*. London and New York

de Jong, I.J.F. (1987) *Narrators and focalizers*. Amsterdam

Joplin, P.K. (1990) 'Ritual work on human flesh: Livy's Lucretia and the rape of the body politic', *Helios* 17: 51–70

Joshel, S.R. (1992) 'The body female and the body politic: Livy's Lucretia and Verginia', in Richlin (1992), 112–30

  (1997) 'Female desire and the discourse of empire: Tacitus's Messalina', in Hallett and Skinner (1997), 221–54

Kahn, C. (1991) '*Lucrèce*: the sexual politics of subjectivity', in Higgins and Silver (1991), 141–59

Kappeler, S. (1986) *The Pornography of Representation*. Minneapolis

Kaster, R.A. (1988) *Guardians of language*. Berkeley

Keith, A.M. (1999) 'Versions of epic masculinity in Ovid's *Metamorphoses*', in P. Hardie, A. Barchiesi, and S.E. Hinds (eds.) *Ovidian transformations*. Cambridge

Kolodny, A. (1975) *The lay of the land*. Chapel Hill

Korn, M. and Tschiedel, H.J. (1991) (eds.) *Ratis omnia uincet: Untersuchungen zu den Argonautica des Valerius Flaccus. Spudasmata* 48. Hildesheim

Koster, S. (1970) *Antike Epostheorien*. Wiesbaden

Kraus, C.S (1991) '*Initium turbandi omnia a femina ortum est:* Fabia Minor and the election of 367 BC', *Phoenix* 45: 314–25

Krevans, N. (1993) 'Ilia's dream: Ennius, Virgil, and the mythology of seduction', *HSCPh* 95: 257–71

Lee, M.O. (1979) *Fathers and sons in Virgil's Aeneid*. Albany

Levitan, W. (1993) 'Give up the beginning? Juno's mindful wrath (*Aeneid* 1.37)', *LCM* 18: 1–15

Loraux, N. (1987) *Tragic ways of killing a woman*, trans. A. Forster. Cambridge, MA and London

  (1995) *The experiences of Tiresias: the feminine and the Greek man*, trans. P. Wissing. Princeton

Lotman, J. (1979) 'The origin of plot in the light of typology', trans. J. Graffy, *Poetics today* 1.1–2, 161–84

Lyne, R.O.A.M. (1983) 'Lavinia's Blush: Vergil, *Aeneid* 12.64–70', *G&R* 30: 55–64

  (1983a) 'Vergil and the politics of war', *CQ* 33: 188–203; reprinted in Harrison (1990), 316–38

  (1987) *Further voices in Vergil's Aeneid*. Oxford

  (1989) *Words and the poet*. Oxford

MacDonald, S., Holden, P., and Ardener, S. (1987) (eds.) *Images of women in peace and war*. London

Malamud, M.A. (1995) '(P)raising the dead in *Silvae* 2.7', in Boyle (1995), 169–98

Malamud, M.A. and McGuire, D.T., Jr. (1993) 'Flavian variant: myth. Valerius' *Argonautica*', in Boyle (1993), 192–217

Maltby, R. (1991) *A lexicon of ancient Latin etymologies*. Leeds

Marcus, J. (1989) 'Corpus/corps/corpse: writing the body in/at war', in Cooper, Munich, and Squier (1989), 124–67

Marrou, H.I. (1956) *A history of education in antiquity*, trans. G. Lamb. London

Marsh, T. (1992) 'The (other) maiden's tale', in Richlin (1992), 269–84

Marshall, A.J. (1989) 'Ladies at law: the role of women in the Roman civil courts', in C. Deroux (ed.), *Studies in Latin literature and Roman history V*: 35–54. Brussels
(1990) 'Women on trial before the Roman senate', *EMC/CV* n.s. 9: 333–66
Martindale, C. (1981) 'Lucan's Hercules: padding or paradigm? A note on *De Bello Civili* 4.589–660', *SO* 56: 71–80
(1997) (ed.) *The Cambridge companion to Virgil.* Cambridge
Marx, K. and Engels, F. (1932) *Die deutsche Ideologie.* Leipzig
Masters, J. (1992) *Poetry and civil war in Lucan's Bellum Civile.* Cambridge
McGuire, D.T. (1990) 'Textual strategies and political suicide in Flavian epic', in Boyle (1990), 21–45
Moi, T. (1990) 'Beauvoir and the intellectual woman', *Yale Journal of Criticism* 4: 1–23
Moles, J. (1984) 'Aristotle and Dido's *hamartia*', *G&R* 31: 48–54
(1987) 'The tragedy and guilt of Dido', in Whitby, Hardie and Whitby (1987), 153–61
Monsacré, H. (1984) *Les larmes d'Achille: le héros, la femme et la souffrance dans la poésie d'Homère.* Paris
Monti, R.C. (1981) *The Dido episode and the Aeneid.* Leiden
Montrose, L. (1991) 'The work of gender in the discourse of discovery', *Representations* 33: 1–41
Muecke, F. (1983) 'Foreshadowing and dramatic irony in the story of Dido', *AJP* 104: 134–55
Murnaghan, S. (1987) *Disguise and recognition in the Odyssey.* Princeton
Myers, K.S. (1994) *Ovid's causes.* Ann Arbor
(1994a) '*Ultimus ardor*: Pomona and Vertumnus in Ovid's *Met.* 14.623–771', *CJ* 89: 225–50
Nagler, M.N. (1990) 'Odysseus: the proem and the problem', *CA* 9: 335–56
Nagy, G. (1979) *The best of the Achaeans.* Baltimore
(1990) *Greek mythology and poetics.* Ithaca
(1990a) *Pindar's Homer: the lyric possession of an epic past.* Baltimore
Nicolet, C. (1991) *Space, geography, and politics in the early Roman empire.* Ann Arbor
Nisbet, R.G.M. (1990) '*Aeneas imperator*: Roman generalship in an epic context', in Harrison (1990), 378–89; reprinted from *PVS* 18 (1978–80): 50–61
Nugent, S.G. (1992) 'Vergil's "voice of the women" in *Aeneid V*', *Arethusa* 25: 255–92
(1994) '*Mater* matters: the female in Lucretius' *De Rerum Natura*', *Colby Quarterly* 30: 179–205
O'Hara, J.J. (1996) *True names: Vergil and the Alexandrian tradition of etymological wordplay.* Ann Arbor
Oliensis, E. (1997) 'Sons and lovers: sexuality and gender in Virgil's poetry', in Martindale (1997), 294–311
Ong, W.J. (1959) 'Latin language study as a renaissance puberty rite', *Studies in Philology* 56: 103–24
(1962) 'Latin and the social fabric', in *The barbarian within, and other fugitive essays and studies*, 206–19. New York
Ortner, S.B. (1974) 'Is female to male as nature is to culture?' in M.Z. Rosaldo and L. Lamphere (eds.), *Woman, culture and society*, 67–87. Stanford

Ortner, S.B. and Whitehead, H. (1981) (eds.) *Sexual meanings: the cultural construction of gender and sexuality*. Cambridge

Ostrowski, J. (1996) 'Personifications of countries and cities as a symbol of victory in Greek and Roman art', in E.G. Schmidt (ed.), *Griechenland und Rom*. Tbilisi.

Otis, B. (1936) 'The argumenta of the so-called Lactantius', *HSCPh* 47: 131–63

(1963) *Virgil: a study in civilized poetry*. Oxford

Parker, P. (1987) *Literary fat ladies: rhetoric, gender, property*. London and New York

Parry, A. (1957) 'Landscape in Greek poetry', *YCS* 15: 3–29

Parry, H. (1964) 'Ovid's *Metamorphoses*: violence in a pastoral landscape', *TAPhA* 95: 268–82

Pearson, L. (1983) *The lost histories of Alexander the Great*. Chico

Pease, A.S. (1935) *P. Vergili Maronis Aeneidos liber quartus*. Cambridge, MA

Peirce, C.S. (1931–58) *Collected papers*, 8 vols. Cambridge, MA

Perkell, C.G. (1981) 'The quality of Aeneas' victory in the *Aeneid*', in Foley (1981), 355–75

Pope, D. (1989) 'Notes toward a supreme fiction: the work of feminist criticism', in J.F. O'Barr (ed.), *Women and a new academy*, 22–37. Madison

Pöschl, V. (1962) *The art of Vergil*, trans. G. Seligson. Ann Arbor.

Powell, A. (1992) (ed.) *Roman poetry and propaganda in the age of Augustus*. London

(1992a) 'The *Aeneid* and the embarrassments of Augustus', in Powell (1992), 141–74.

Putnam, M.C.J. (1994) 'Virgil's Danaid ekphrasis', *ICS* 19: 171–89

(1995) *Virgil's Aeneid: interpretation and influence*. Chapel Hill and London

Quint, D. (1993) *Epic and empire*. Princeton

Rabel, R.J. (1985) 'The Harpies in the *Aeneid*', *CJ* 80: 317–25

Rabinowitz, N.S. (1992) 'Tragedy and the politics of containment', in Richlin (1992), 36–52

(1993) *Anxiety veiled: Euripides and the traffic in women*. Ithaca

Rand, E.K. *et al.* (1946) *Servianorum in Vergilii carmina commentariorum, vol. II.* Lancaster

Rawson, E. (1975) *Cicero: a portrait*. Ithaca

Reckford, K.J. (1961) 'Latent tragedy in *Aeneid* VII, 1–285', *AJP* 82: 252–69

Rehm, R. (1994) *Marriage to death*. Princeton

Rich, J. & Shipley, G. (1993) *War and society in the Roman world*. New York and London

Richlin A. (1984) 'Invective against women in Roman satire', *Arethusa* 17: 67–80

(1992) (ed.) *Pornography and representation in Greece and Rome*. Oxford

(1992a) 'Reading Ovid's rapes', in Richlin (1992), 158–79

(1992b) 'Making gender in the Roman forum', *APA Abstracts*, 152

(1992c) *The garden of Priapus: sexuality and aggression in Roman humor*, 2nd edn. Oxford

Rose, G. (1993) *Feminism and geography*. Minneapolis

Rubin, G. (1975) 'The traffic in women: notes toward a political economy of sex', in R. Reiter (ed.), *Toward an anthropology of women*, 157–210. New York

Said, E.W. (1993) *Culture and imperialism*. New York

Sartori, P. (1898) 'Über das Bauopfer', *Zeitschrift für Ethnologie* 13: 1–54

Scarry, E. (1985) *The body in pain*. New York and Oxford

Schein, S.L. (1984) *The mortal hero*. Berkeley, Los Angeles and London

Sedgwick, E.K. (1985) *Between men: English literature and male homosocial desire*. New York

Segal, C.P. (1968) 'Circean temptations: Homer, Vergil, Ovid', *TAPhA* 99: 419–42

(1969) *Landscape in Ovid's Metamorphoses: a study in the transformations of a literary symbol. Hermes Einzelschriften* 23. Wiesbaden

Sinclair, P. (1995) *The sententious historian: a sociology of rhetoric in* 'Annales' *1–6*. University Park

Skutsch, O. (1985) *The Annals of Quintus Ennius*. Oxford

Slatkin, L.M. (1991) *The power of Thetis*. Berkeley, Los Angeles and Oxford

Starr, R.J. (1991) 'Explaining Dido to your son: Tiberius Claudius Donatus on Vergil's Dido', *CJ* 87: 25–34

Stehle, E. (1989) 'Venus, Cybele, and the Sabine women: the Roman construction of female sexuality', *Helios* 16: 143–64

Stocker, A.R. *et al.* (1965) *Servianorum in Vergilii carmina commentariorum, vol. III.* Lancaster

Suleiman, S.R. (1986) (ed.) *The female body in western culture*. Cambridge MA and London

Thilo, G. and Hagen, H. (1884) *Servii Grammatici qui feruntur in Vergilii carmina commentarii*. Leipzig; repr. Hildesheim, 1961

Toynbee, J.M.C. (1934) *The Hadrianic school: a chapter in the history of Greek art*. Cambridge

Vance, E. (1973) 'Warfare and the structure of thought in Virgil's *Aeneid*', *QUCC* 15: 111–62

van der Graaf, C. (1945) *The Dirae, with translation, commentary and an investigation of its authorship*. Leiden

Vernant, J.-P (1991) 'A "beautiful death" and the disfigured corpse in Homeric epic', in F.I. Zeitlin (ed.), *Mortals and immortals: collected essays of Jean-Pierre Vernant*, 50–74. Princeton

Versnel, H.S (1976) 'Two types of Roman *deuotio*', *Mnem.* 29: 365–410

Vessey, D.W.T. (1970) 'Notes on the Hypsipyle episode in Statius, *Thebaid* 4–6', *BICS* 17: 44–54

(1973) *Statius and the Thebaid*. Cambridge

Whitby, M., Hardie, P., and Whitby, M. (1987) *Homo viator: classical essays for John Bramble*. Bristol and Oak Park

Wiedemann, T. (1992) *Emperors and gladiators*. London and New York

Wilkins, J. (1990) 'The state and the individual: Euripides' plays of voluntary self-sacrifice', in A. Powell (ed.), *Euripides, women and sexuality*, 177–94. London and New York

Williams, G.W. (1983) *Technique and Ideas in the Aeneid*. New Haven

Wiltshire, S.F. (1989) *Private and public in Virgil's Aeneid*. Amherst

Winkler, J.J. (1990) *The constraints of desire*. New York

Wiseman, T.P. (1995) *Remus. A Roman myth*. Cambridge

Wittig, M. (1986) 'The mark of gender', in N.K. Miller (ed.), *The poetics of gender*, 63–73. New York

Woolf, G. (1993) 'Roman peace', in Rich and Shipley (1993), 171–94

Wyke, M. (1989) 'Mistress and metaphor in Augustan elegy', *Helios* 16: 25–47

(1992) 'Augustan Cleopatras: female power and poetic authority', in Powell (1992), 98–140

(1995) 'Taking the woman's part: engendering Roman love elegy', in Boyle (1995), 110–28

Zanker, P. (1988) *The power of images in the age of Augustus.* Ann Arbor

General index

Index of passages discussed